Smiths Falls Ontario in Colour Photos, Saving Our History One Photo at a Time

Photography
by Barbara Raué
2016

Series Name:
Cruising Ontario

Book 159: Smiths Falls

Cover photo: 16 Maple Avenue, Page 31

Series Name: Cruising Ontario
Saving Our History One Photo at a Time
in colour photos

Books Available in Alphabetical Order:
Aberfoyle, Acton, Alton, Amherstburg, Ancaster, Arthur, Aylmer, Ayr, Bloomingdale, Brantford, Burlington, Caledon, Caledonia, Cambridge, Clifford, Conestogo, Delhi, Dorchester to Aylmer, Drayton, Drumbo, Dundas, Eden Mills, Elmira, Elora, Essex, Fergus, Guelph, Hagersville, Hamilton, Hanover, Harriston, Hespeler, Jarvis, Kingston, Kingsville, Kitchener, Linwood, Listowel, London, Lucknow, Mono, Mount Forest, Neustadt, New Hamburg, Niagara-on-the-Lake, Oakville, Orangeville, Orillia, Owen Sound, Palmerston, Peterborough, Petrolia, Port Elgin, Preston, Rockwood, Sarnia, Seaforth, Sheffield, Shelburne, Simcoe, Southampton, St. Jacobs, St. Marys, St. Thomas, Stoney Creek, Stratford, Thamesford, Tillsonburg, Waterdown, Waterford, Waterloo, Welland, Wellesley, Windsor, Wingham, Woodstock

Other Books by Barbara Raue

Coins of Gold

Arrows, Indians and Love

The Life and Times of Barbara
Volume 1: Inventions That Have Enhanced My Life
Volume 2: Entertainment That I Have Enjoyed
Volume 3: East Coast Trips
Volume 4: Olympics Have Always Intrigued Me
Volume 5: Wonders of the World
Volume 6: Caribbean Cruises We Have Enjoyed
Volume 7: Animals
Volume 8: Storms and Other Major Disasters in My Lifetime
Volume 9: Wars, Terrorist Attacks and Major Disasters

The Cromwell Family Book

Laura Secord Discovered

Daddy Where Are You?

Montana Series
Book 1: Montana Dream
Book 2: Life on the Montana Frontier
Book 3: Montana to Boston and Back

Visit Barbara's website to view all of her books
http://barbararaue.ca

Table of Contents

Smiths Falls is a town in Eastern Ontario located fourteen miles east of Perth. The Rideau Canal waterway passes through the town, with four separate locks in three locations and a combined lift of over fifteen metres (fifty feet). The city is named after Thomas Smyth, a United Empire Loyalist who in 1786 was granted 400 acres here. In 1846, there were fifty dwellings, two grist mills (one with four run of stones), two sawmills, one carding and fulling mill, seven stores, six groceries, one axe factory, six blacksmiths, two wheelwrights, one cabinet maker, one chair-maker, three carpenters, one gunsmith, eleven shoemakers, seven tailors, one tinsmith and two taverns.

At the time of construction of the Rideau Canal a small settlement had been established around a mill operated by Abel Russell Ward, who had bought Smyth's land. Colonel By ordered the removal of Ward's mill to make way for the canal. The disruption of industry caused by the building of the canal was only temporary, and Smiths Falls grew rapidly following construction.

The Rideau Canal area is home to a variety of ecosystems. The land along the Rideau that was once logged is now home to deep-rooted deciduous and coniferous forests that have been maturing for over one hundred years. Where the landscape flattens, there are cedar/hardwood swamps, bogs and cattail marshes which support the healthy wildlife population.

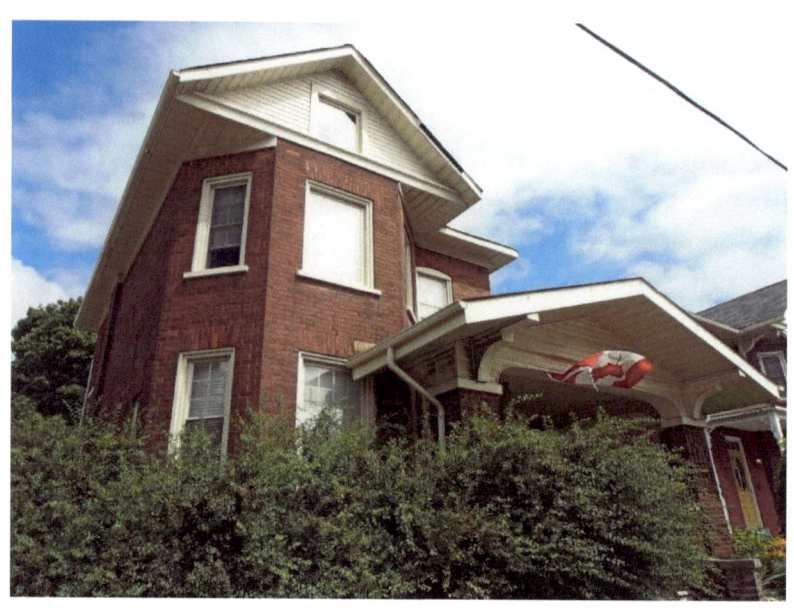

129 Elmsley Street North - Vernacular

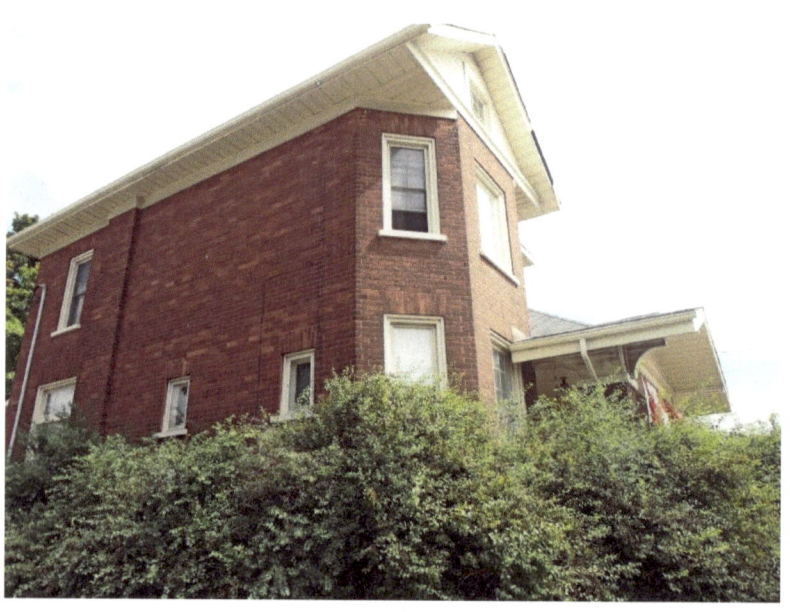

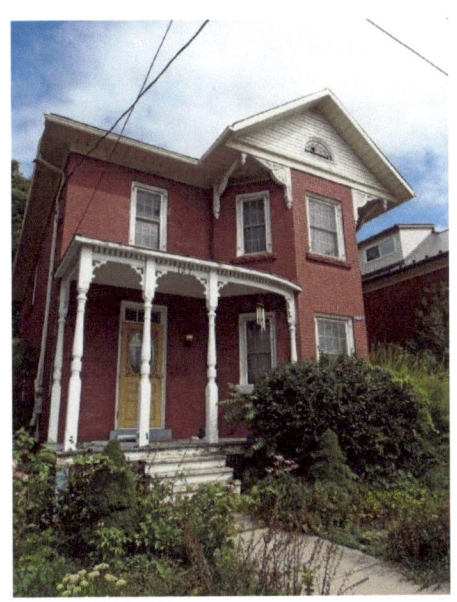

127 Elmsley Street North – two-storey tower-like bay with pediment and fretwork; turned veranda roof supports with decorative capitals

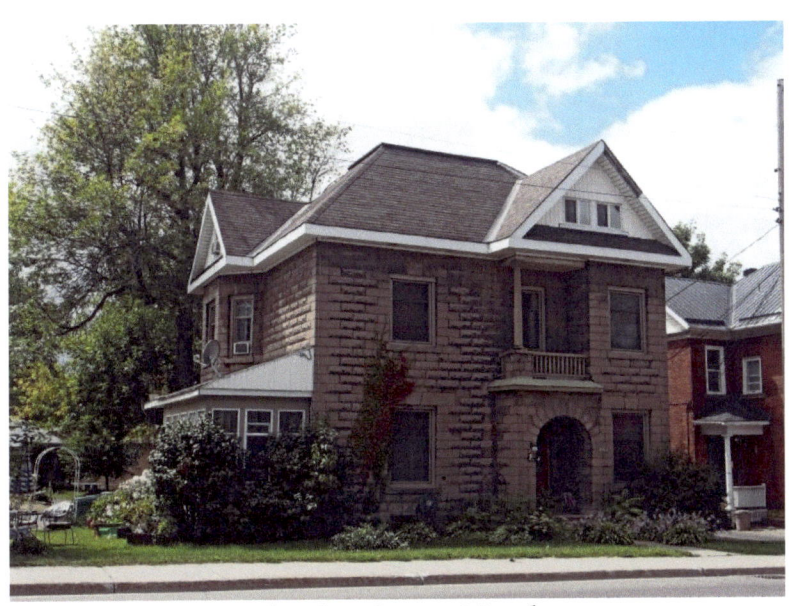

Elmsley Street North

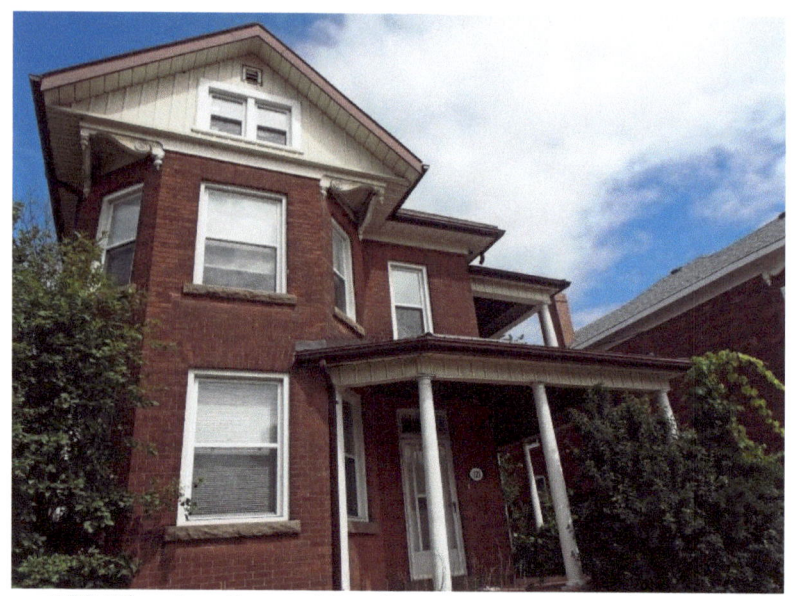

123 Elmsley Street North – Vernacular - fretwork

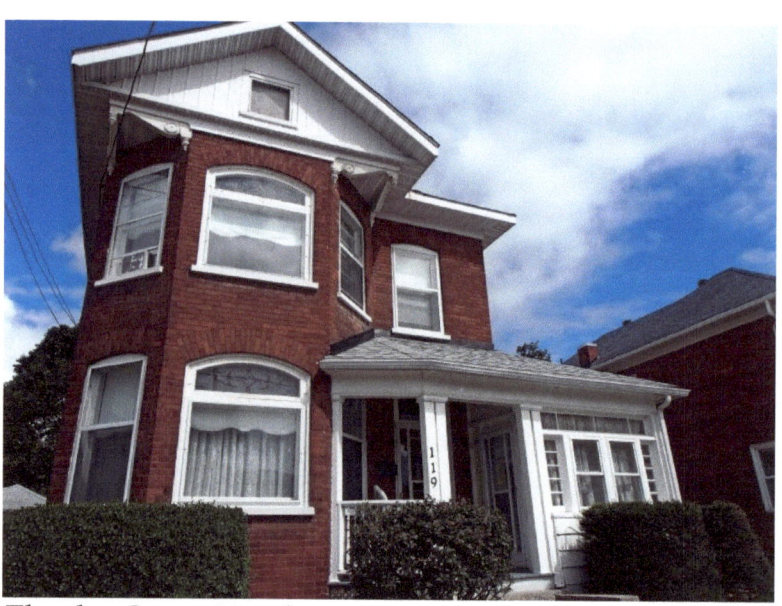

119 Elmsley Street North – Vernacular - two-storey tower-like bay with pediment and fretwork

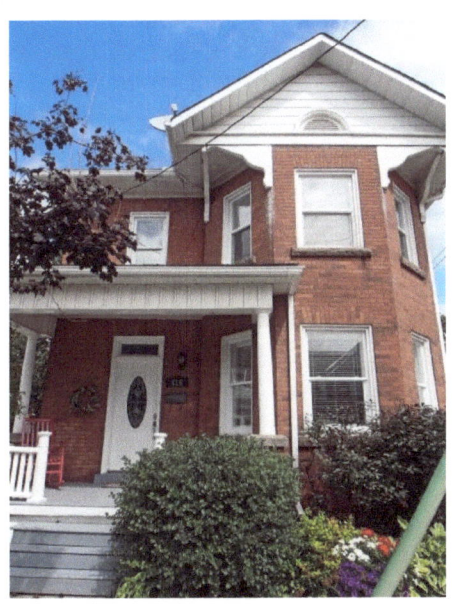

115 Elmsley Street North – Vernacular - two-storey tower-like bay with pediment and fretwork

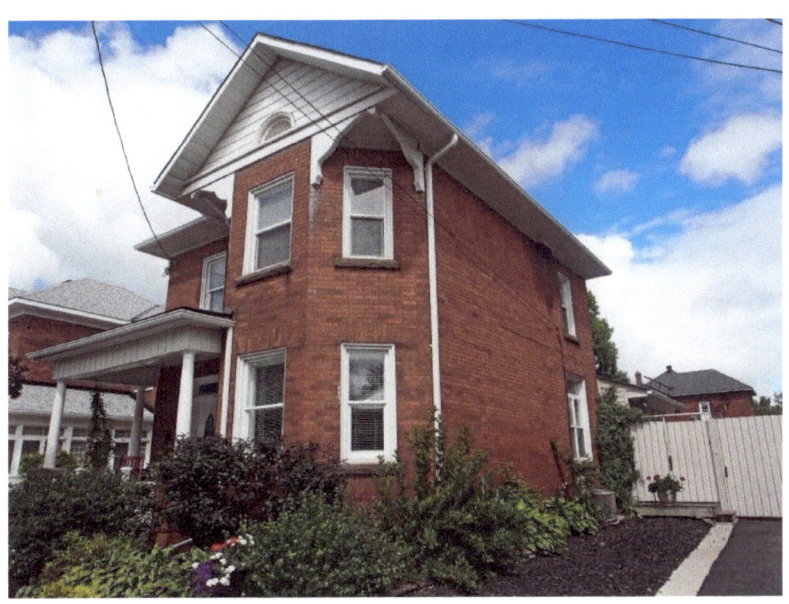

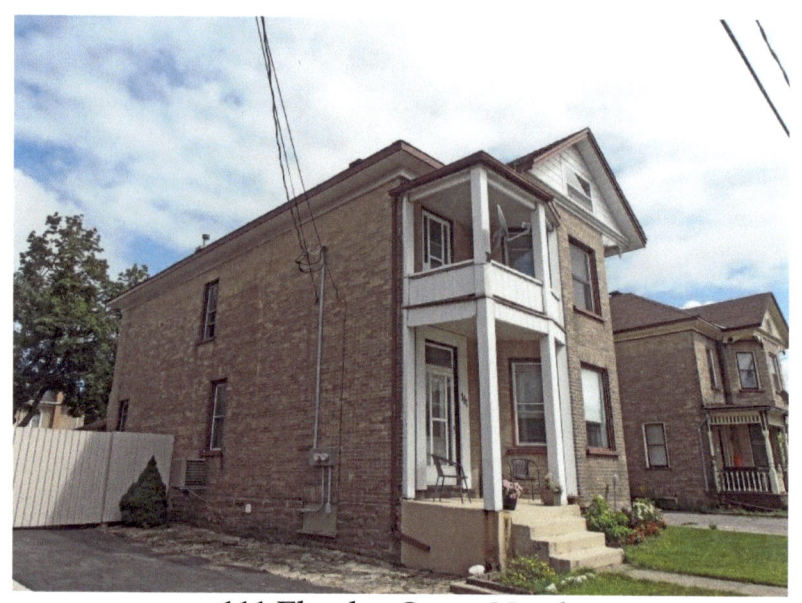

111 Elmsley Street North

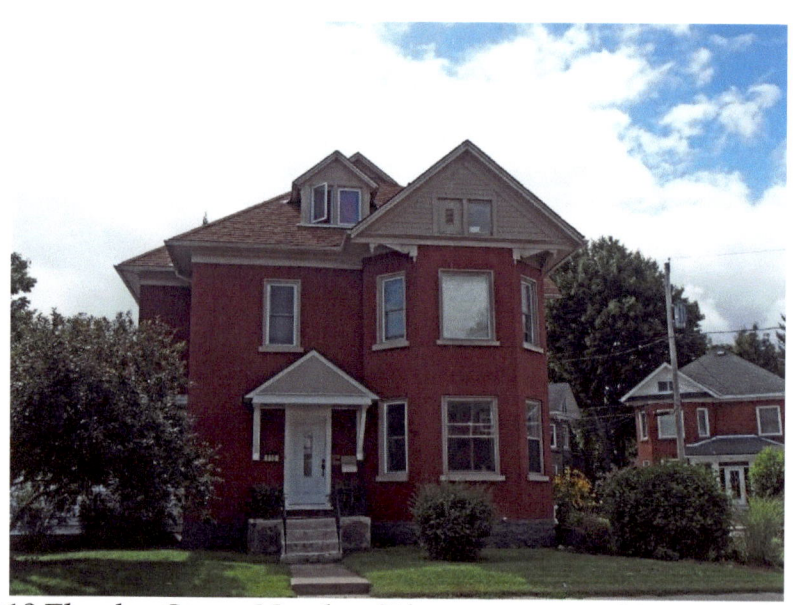

110 Elmsley Street North – 2½-storey tower-like bay with pediment and fretwork; dormer

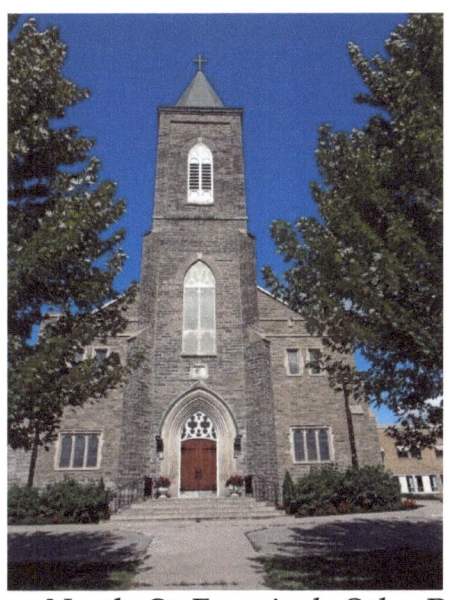

17 Elmsley Street North, St. Francis de Sales Roman Catholic
Church – Gothic Revival – buttresses, lancet windows

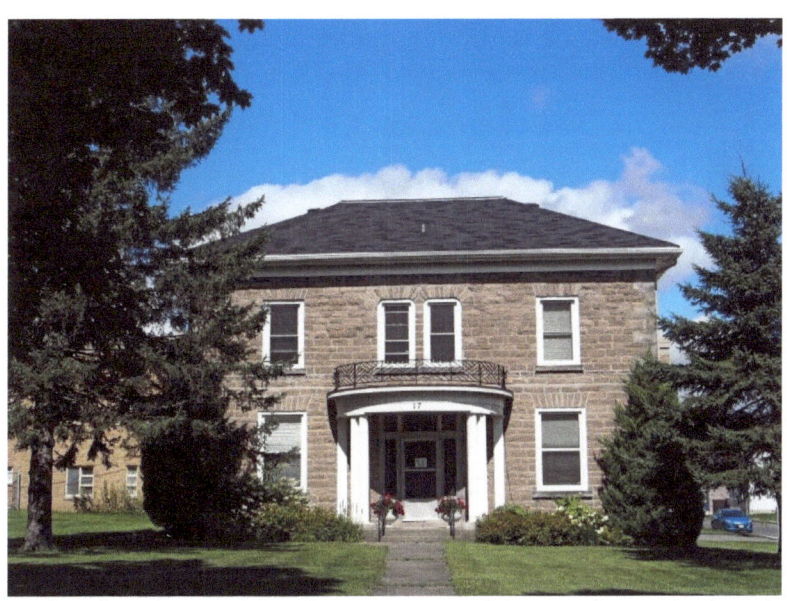

17 Elmsley Street North – manse – hip roof, semi-circular
balcony above porch

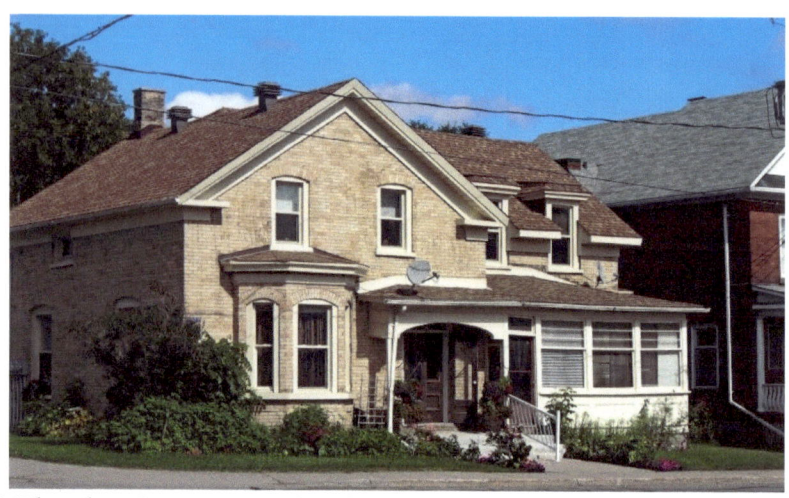

15 Elmsley Street North – former home of James Shaw, first senator of Smiths Falls - Gothic – cornice return on gable, bay window

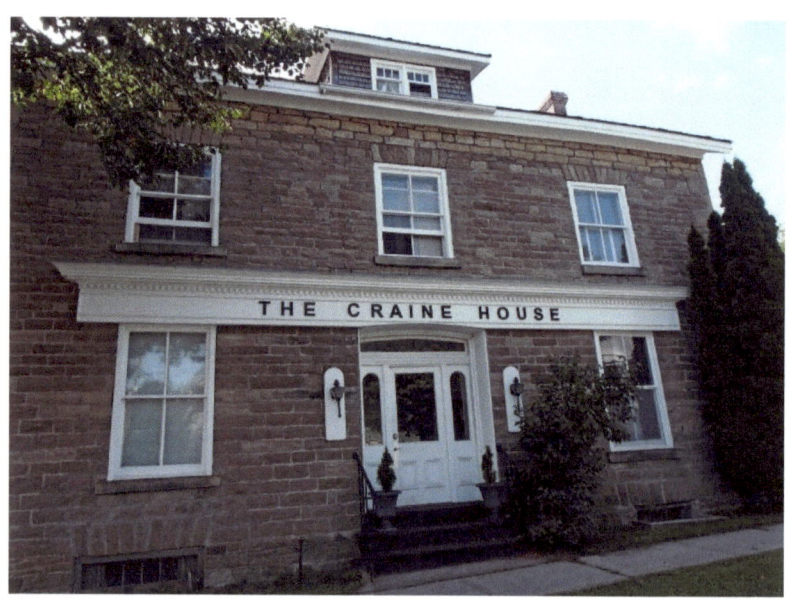

THE CRAINE HOUSE

2 Bay Street North – The Craine House – home of one of Canada's first women doctors - dormer

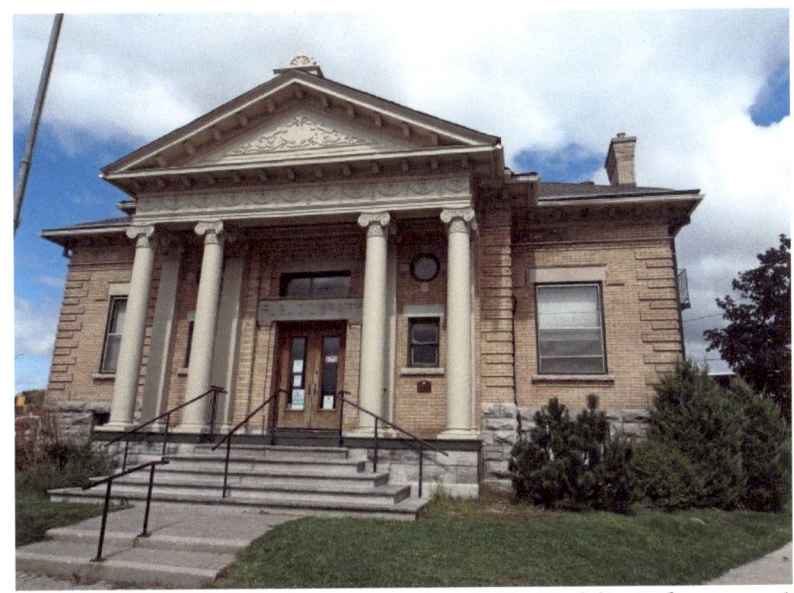

81 Beckwith Street North – Smiths Falls Public Library – 1903
– Beaux Arts style, Ionic pillars supporting pediment with
decorated tympanum and decorative cornice; corner quoins

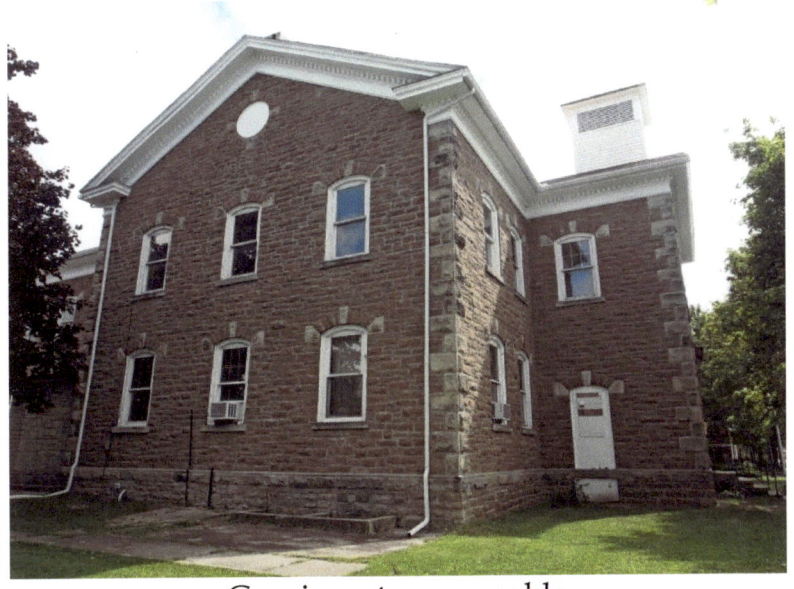

Cornice return on gable

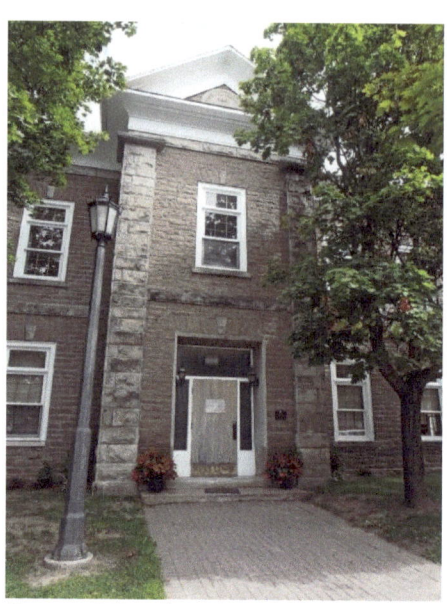

79 Beckwith Street North – Town Hall – 1859 – Classical Revival style – well-proportioned façade, evenly spaced windows

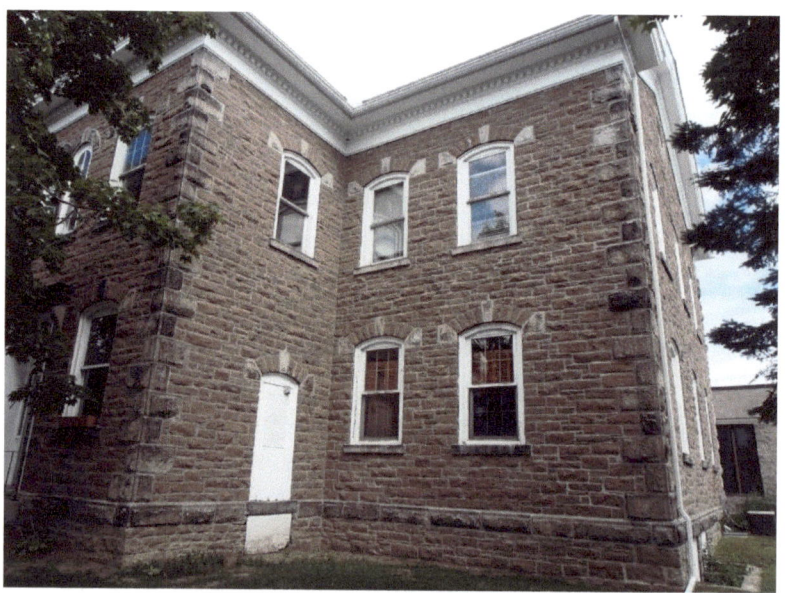

Voussoirs, keystones, dentil molding, quoins, string courses

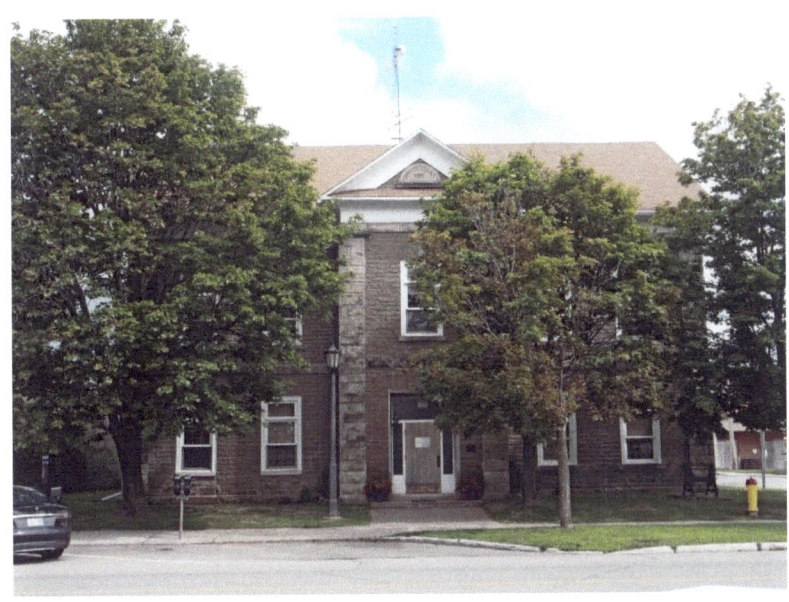

79 Beckwith Street North – former Central School – 1871 –
Classical Revival style – well-proportioned façade, evenly
spaced windows

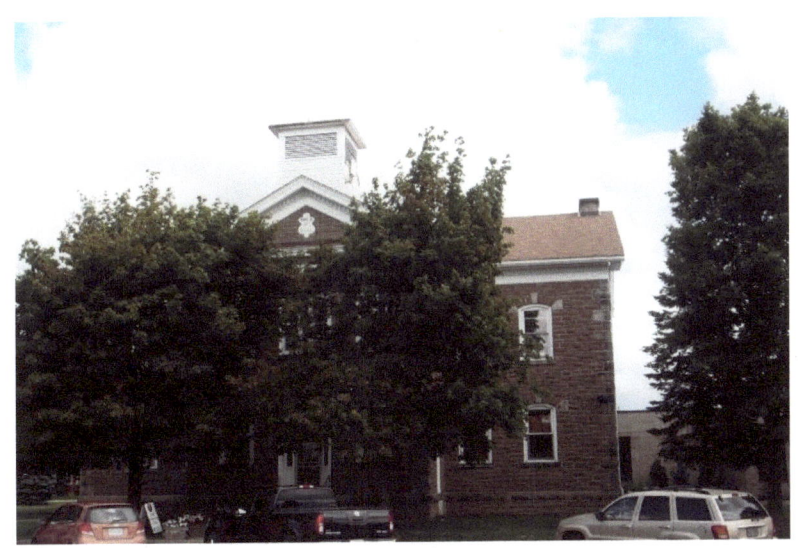

Cupola

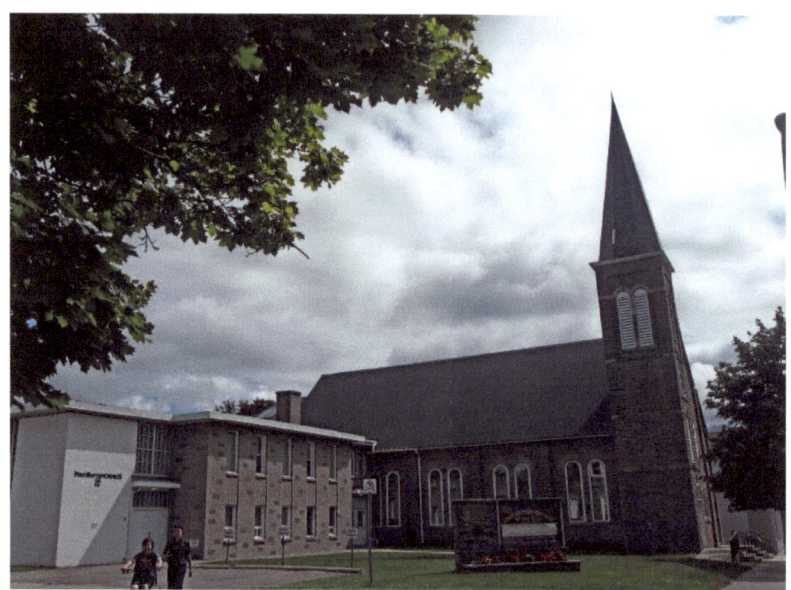

73 Beckwith Street North – First Baptist Church - 1873

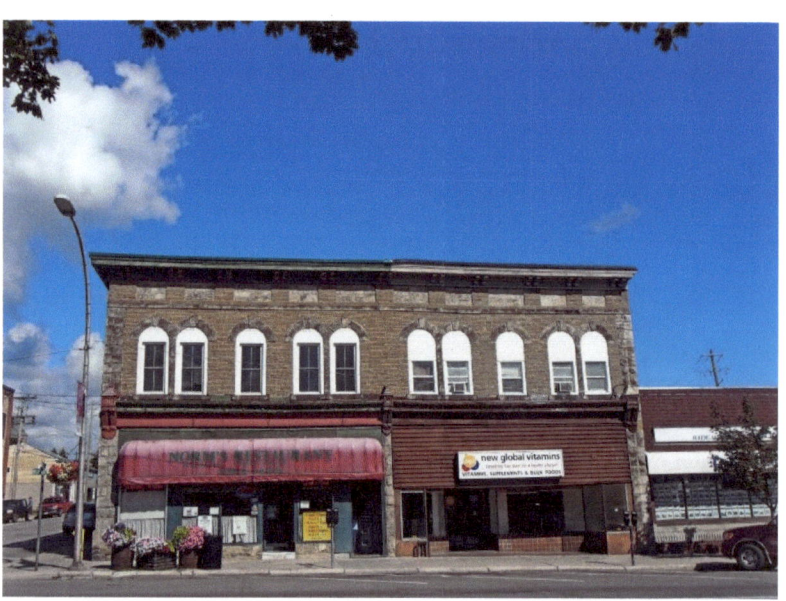

27 Beckwith Street North – paired cornice brackets, dichromatic brickwork, keystones, corner quoins

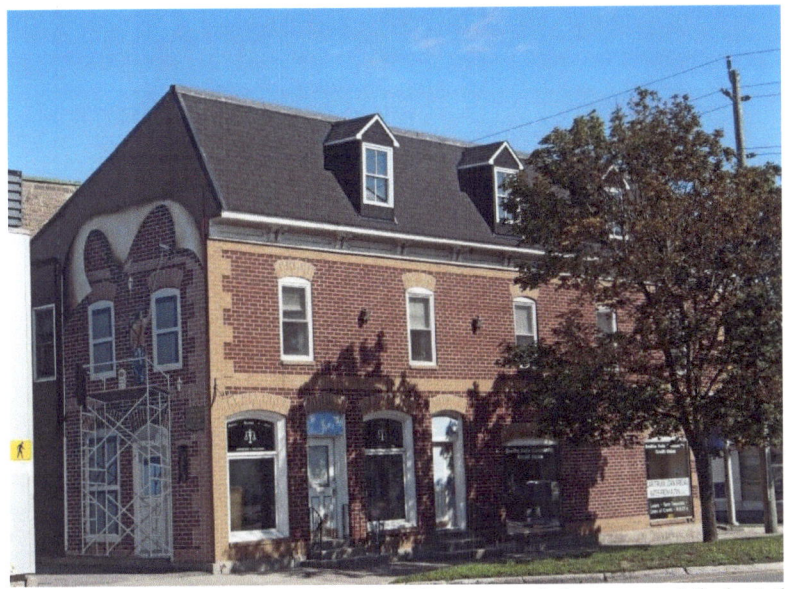

1 Beckwith Street North – 1880 – wood frame with brick veneer, dormers; dichromatic quoins, voussoirs, and banding

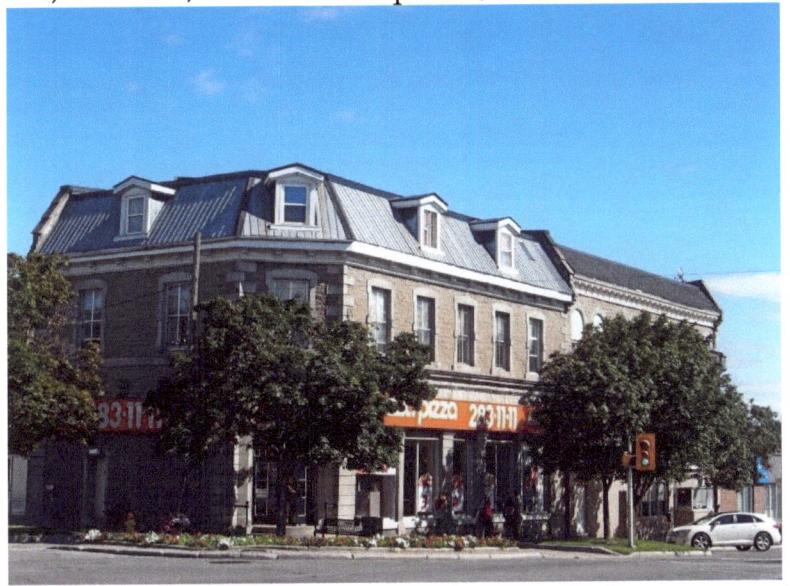

1 Beckwith Street South – corner of Main – light stone quoins, large oval topped windows, dormers

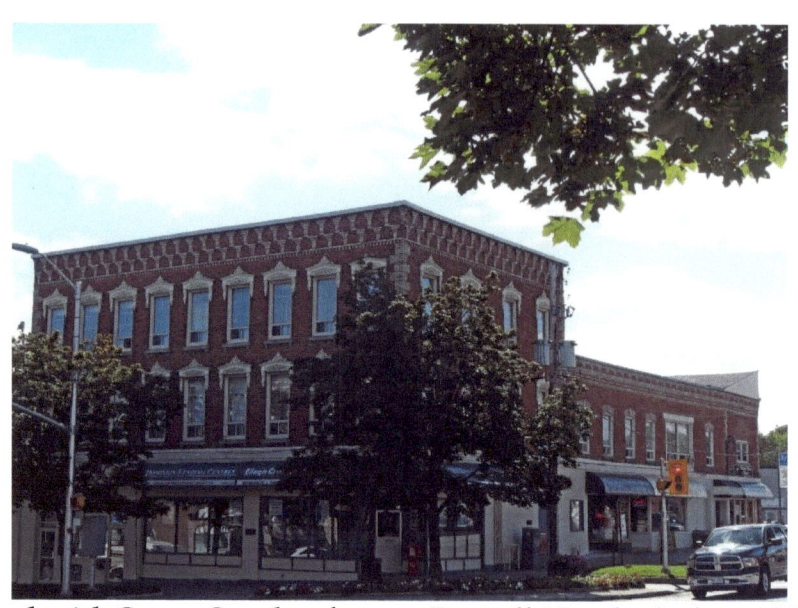

2 Beckwith Street South – former Russell Hotel – before 1885 it was called Wardrobe Hotel – decorative cornice, window hoods, corner quoins

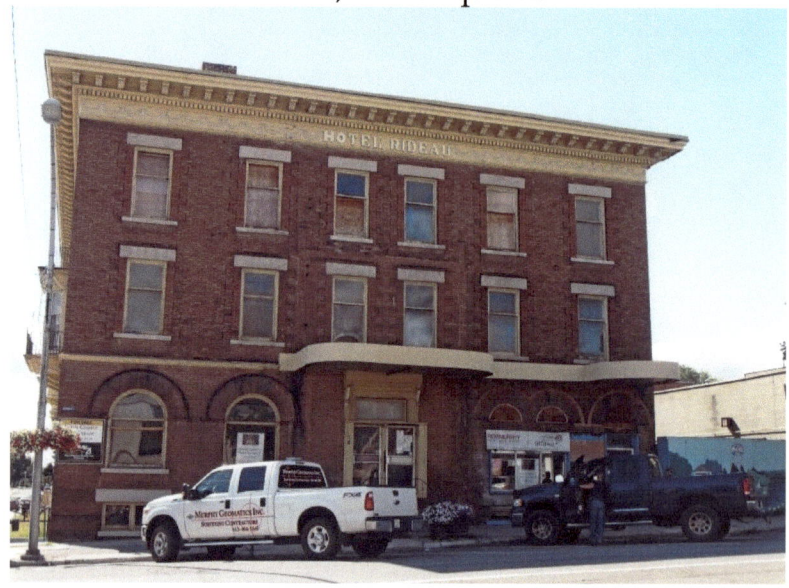

20 Beckwith Street South – Hotel Rideau – 1901 – dentil moulding, window quoins

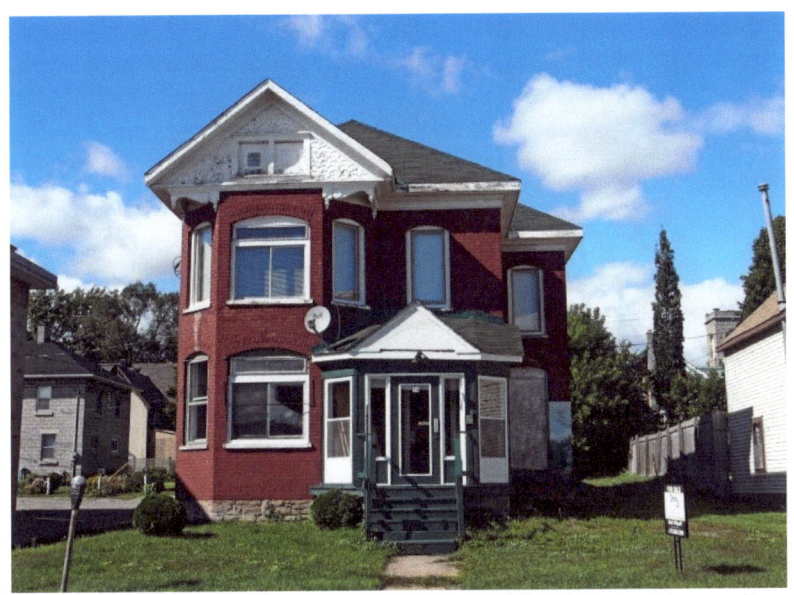

14 Beckwith Street - 2½-storey tower-like bay with pediment and fretwork; pediment above enclosed porch

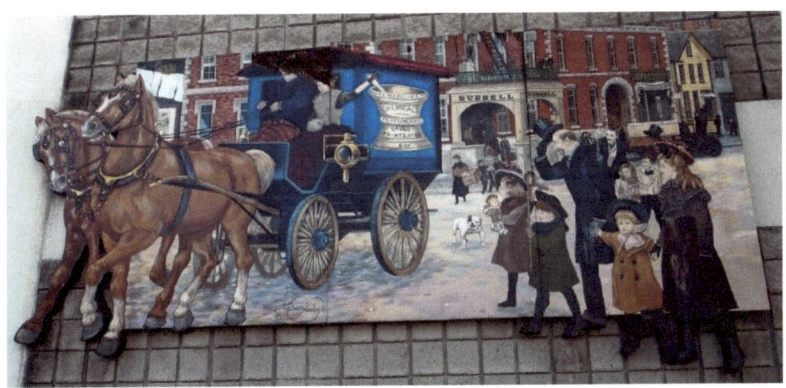

Mural

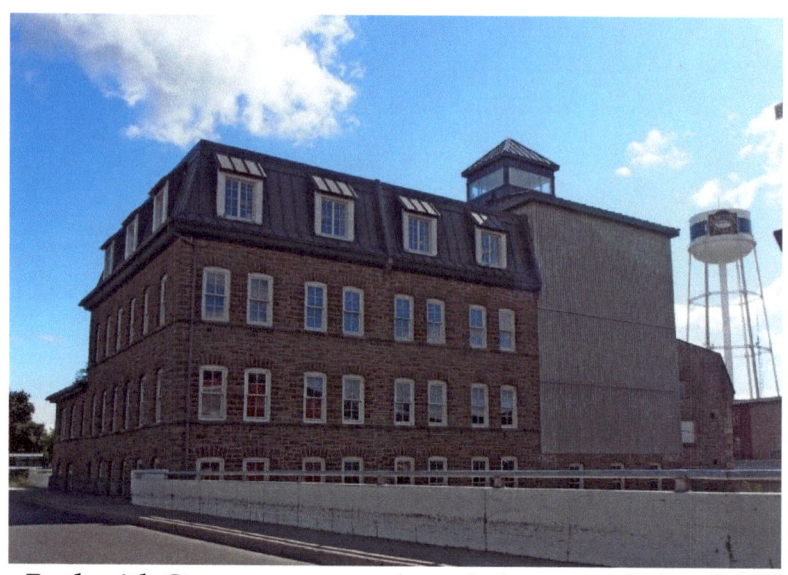

Beckwith Street – mansard roof, dormers, belvedere

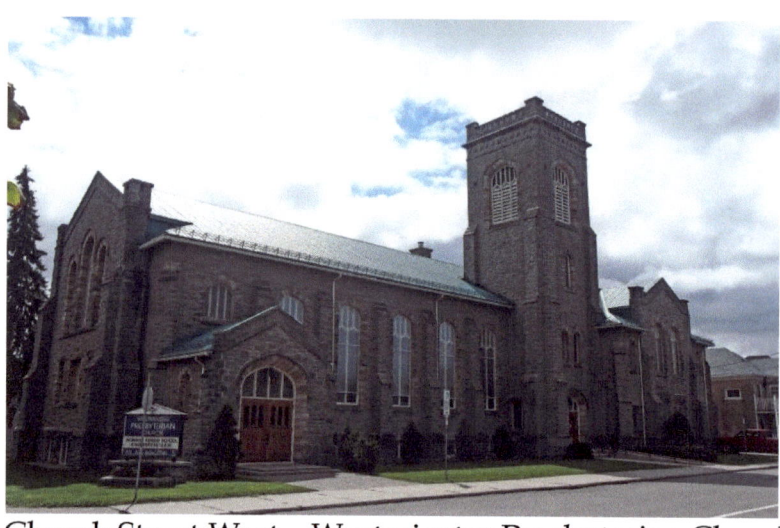

11 Church Street West – Westminster Presbyterian Church –
1928 – Romanesque – rounded windows, buttresses, square
battlemented tower

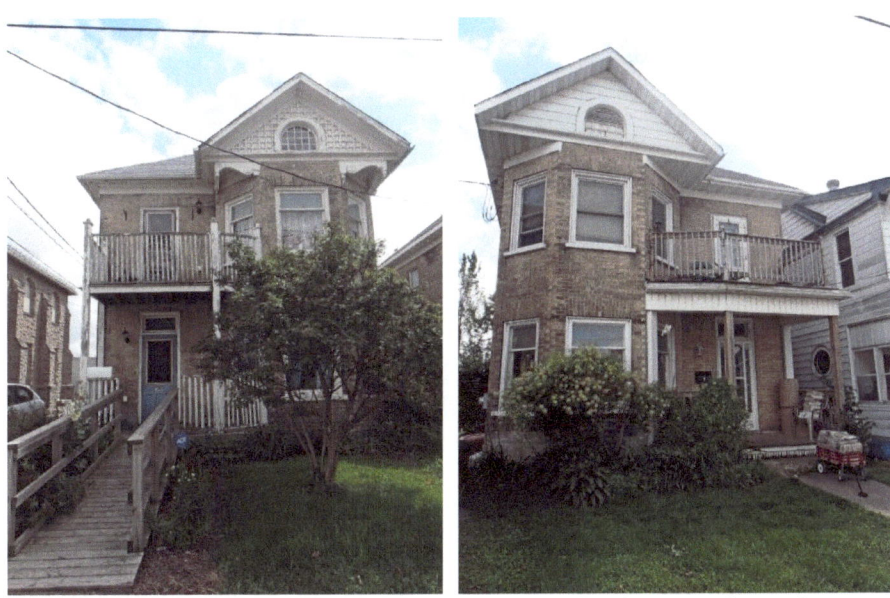

Church Street West - 2½-storey tower-like bay with pediment and fretwork; second floor balcony

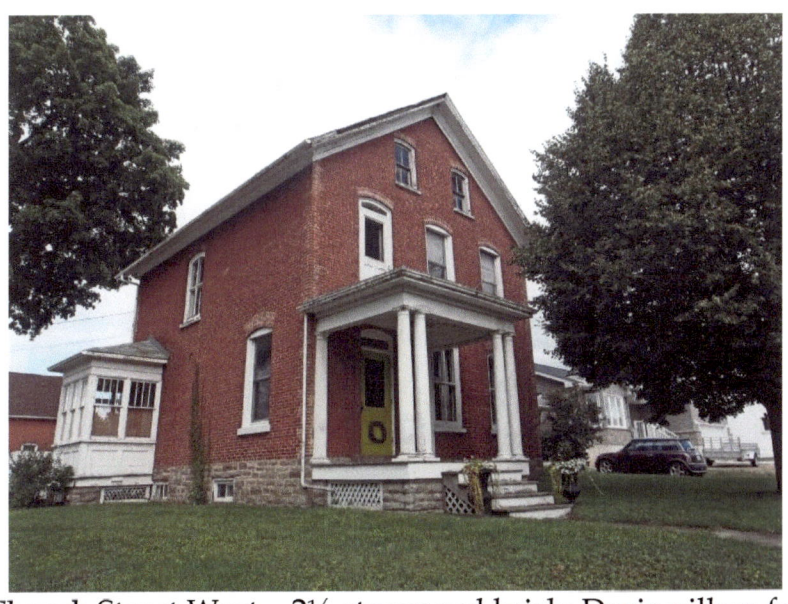

Church Street West – 2½ storey red brick; Doric pillars for porch supports; bay window on side

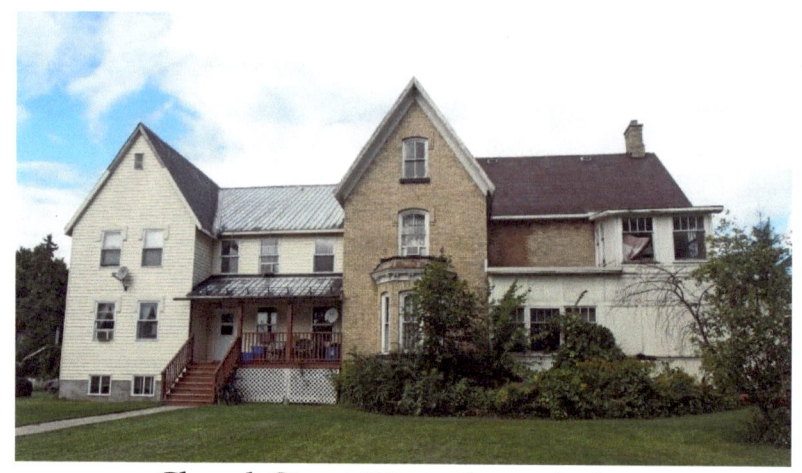

Church Street West – bay window

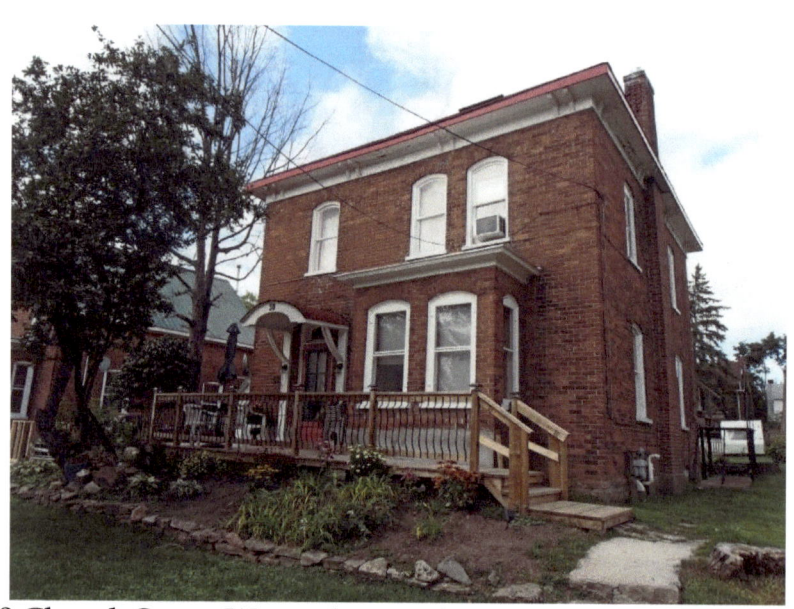

30 Church Street West – hip roof, rectangular bay window

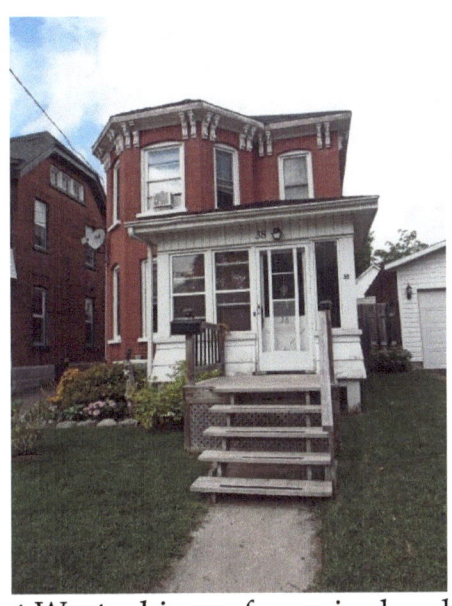

38 Church Street West – hip roof, cornice brackets; two-storey bay window

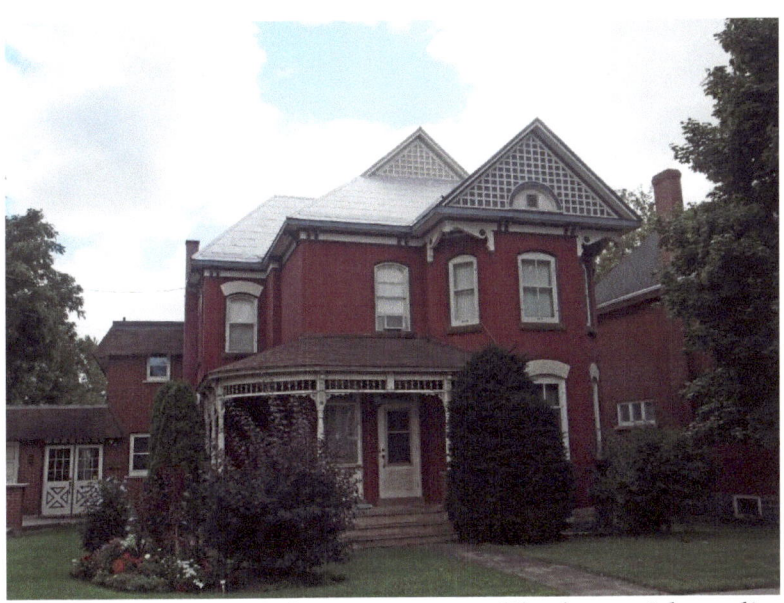

Church Street West - 2½-storey tower-like bay with pediment and fretwork; wraparound veranda with decorative capitals on pillars and spindles

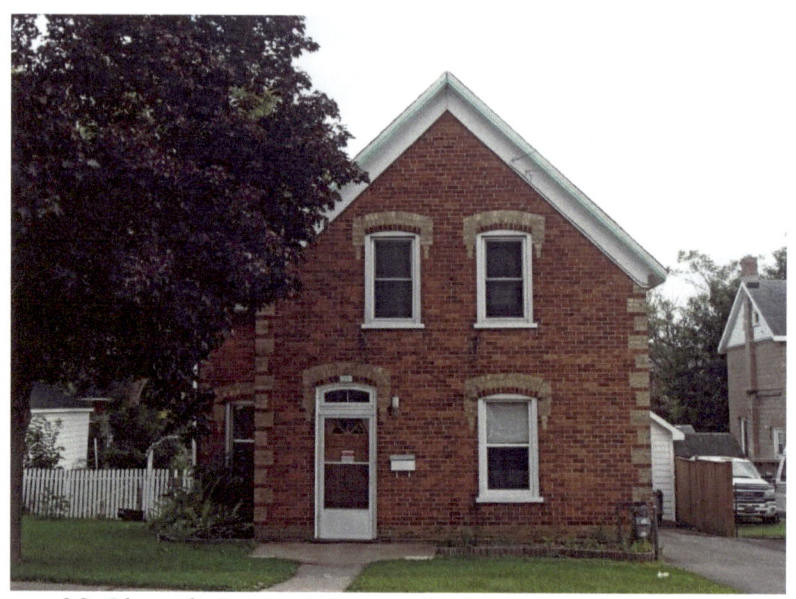

39 Church Street West – Gothic – corner quoins

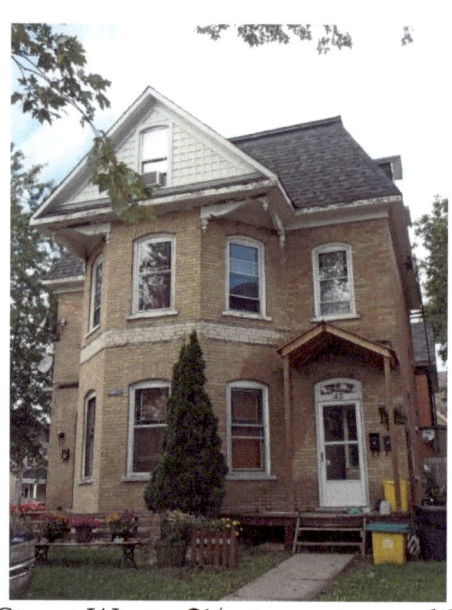

42 Church Street West - 2½-storey tower-like bay with
pediment and fretwork

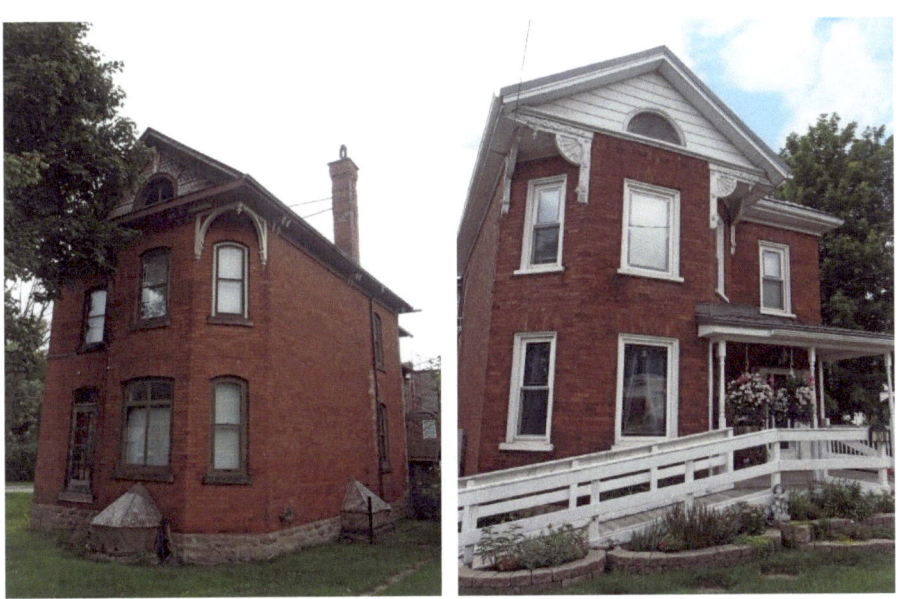

George Street North – 2½ storey tower-like bay with semi-circular window in gable which is supported with fretwork

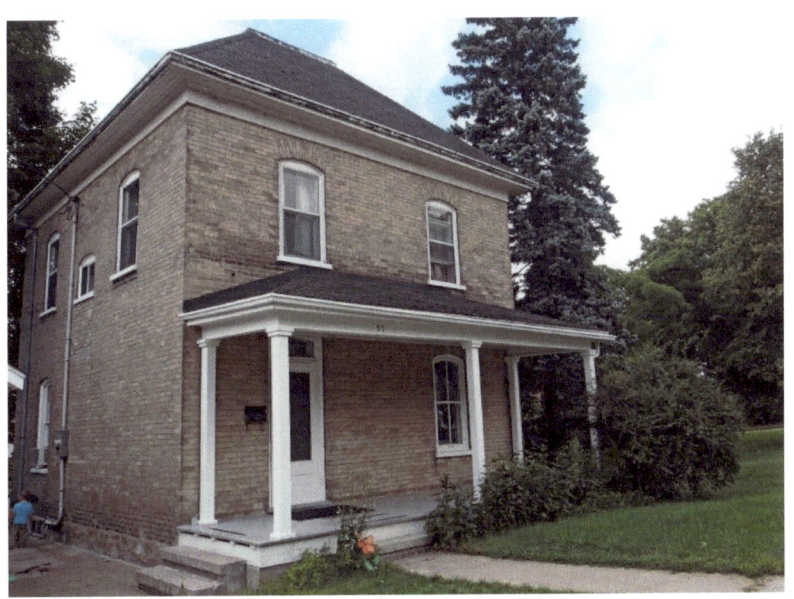

32 George Street North – hip roof

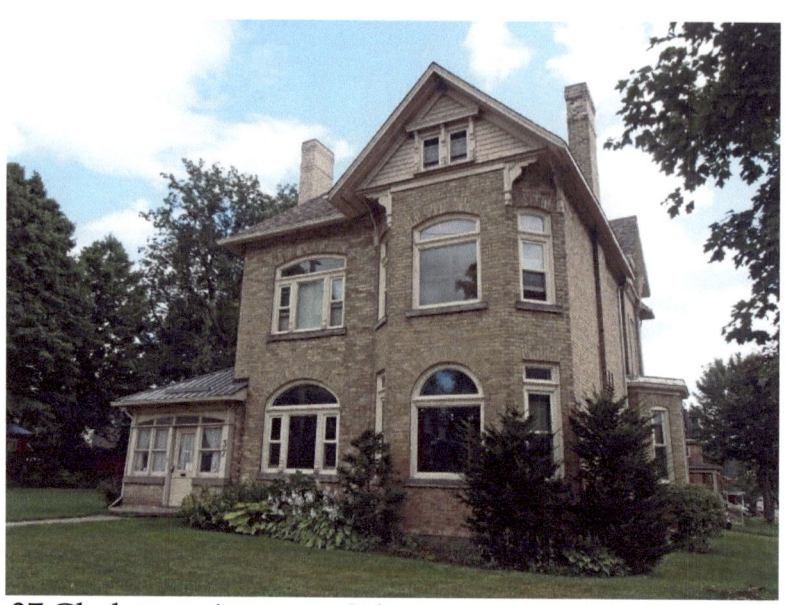

37 Gladstone Avenue - 2½-storey tower-like bay with pediment and fretwork; bay window on side

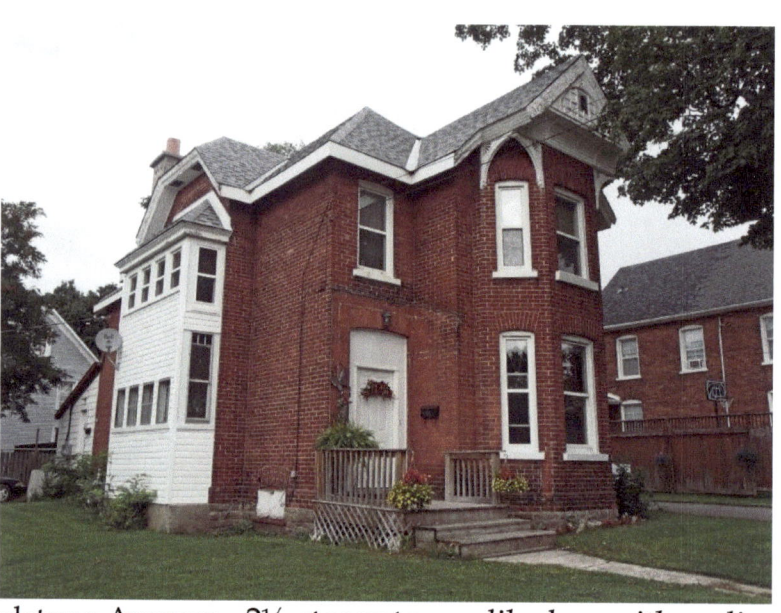

Gladstone Avenue - 2½-storey tower-like bay with pediment and fretwork

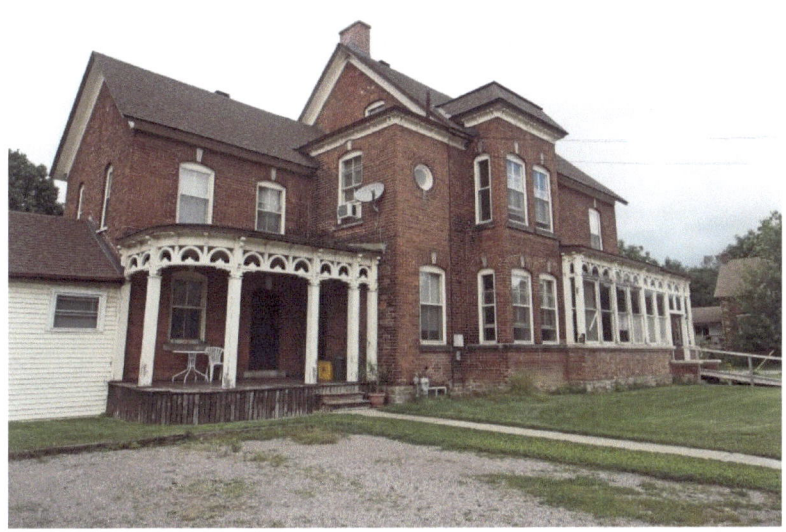

Gladstone Avenue – Queen Anne style – various roof angles; voussoirs, keystones; two-storey tower-like bay; pillars with decorative capitals and trim under roof on open verandah and enclosed porch

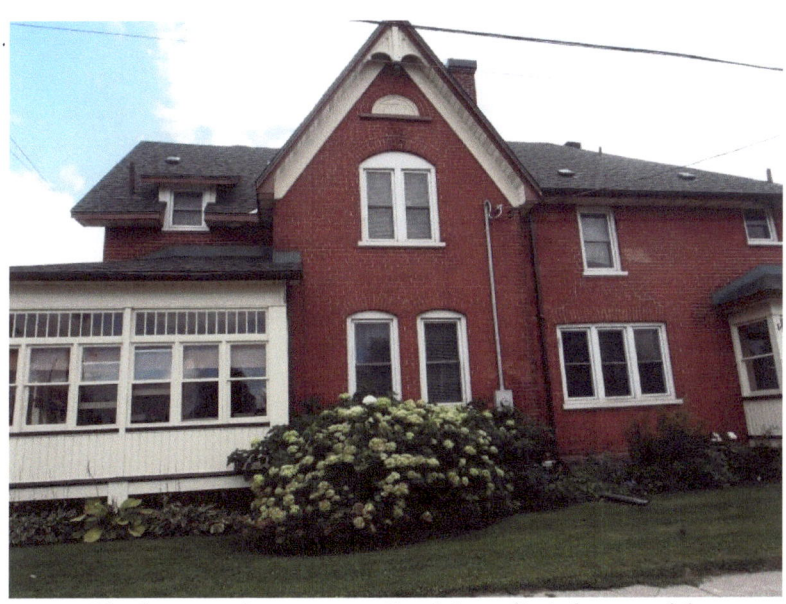

Gladstone Avenue – Gothic – finial on gable

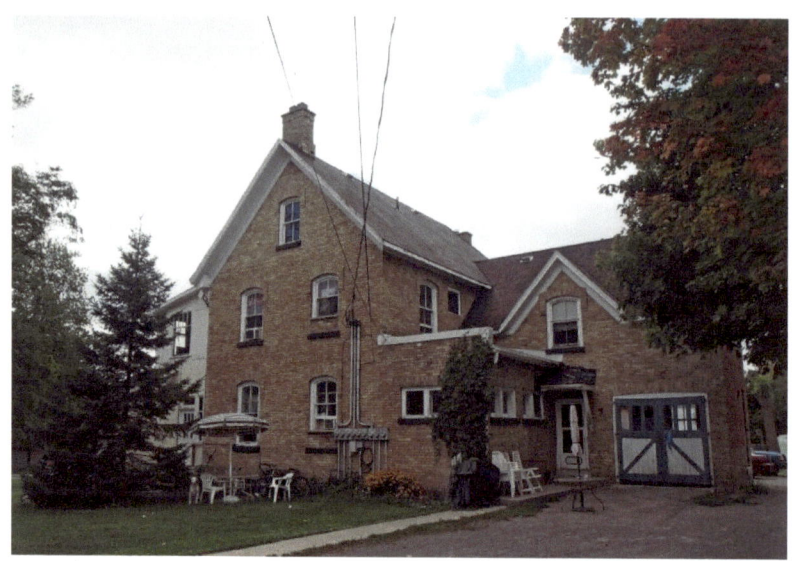

30 Maple Avenue – Gothic – 2½ storeys with 1½ storey wing

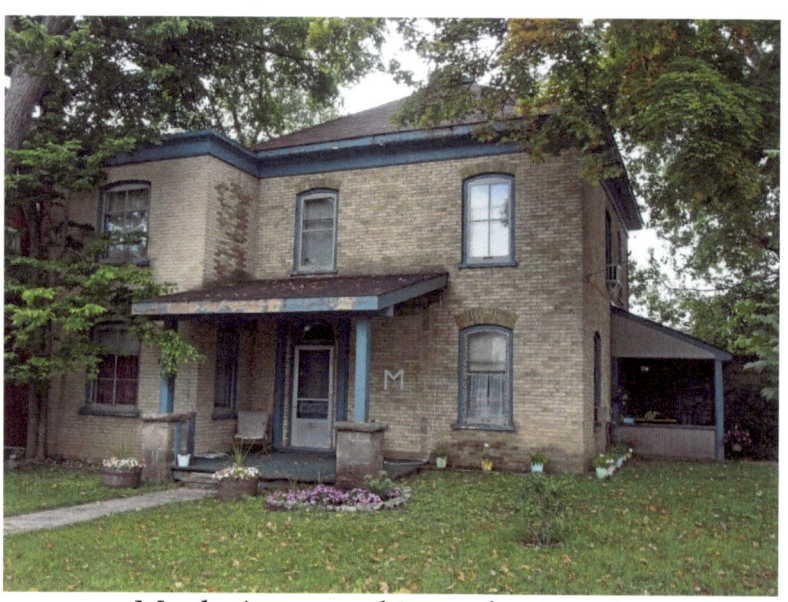

Maple Avenue – hip roof, voussoirs

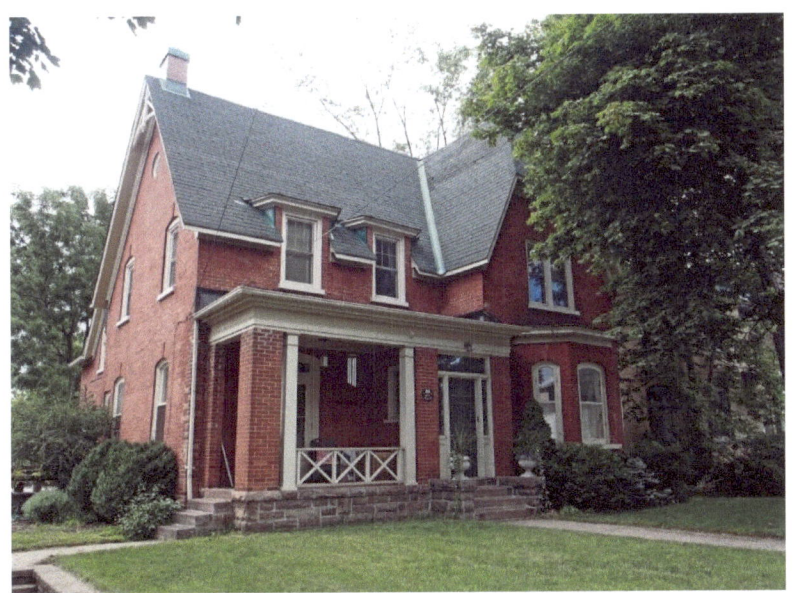

26 Maple Avenue – trim at top of end gable, bay window

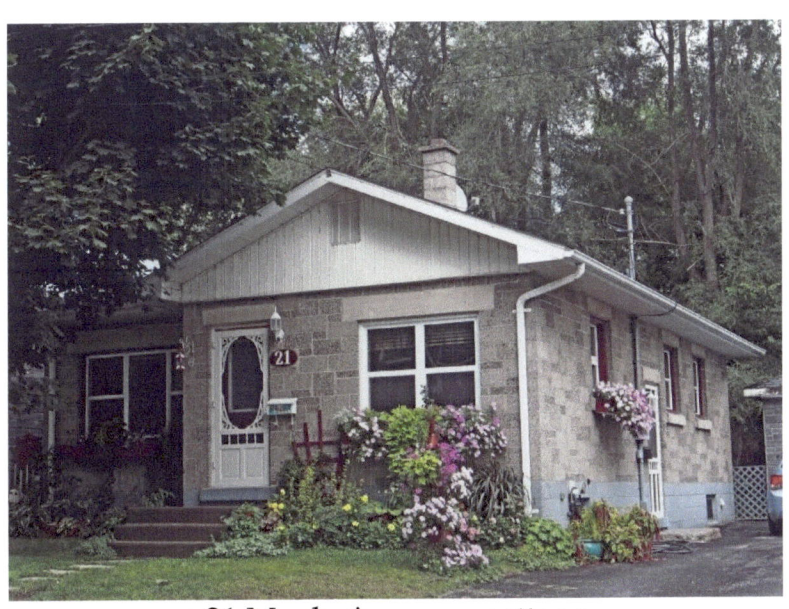

21 Maple Avenue - cottage

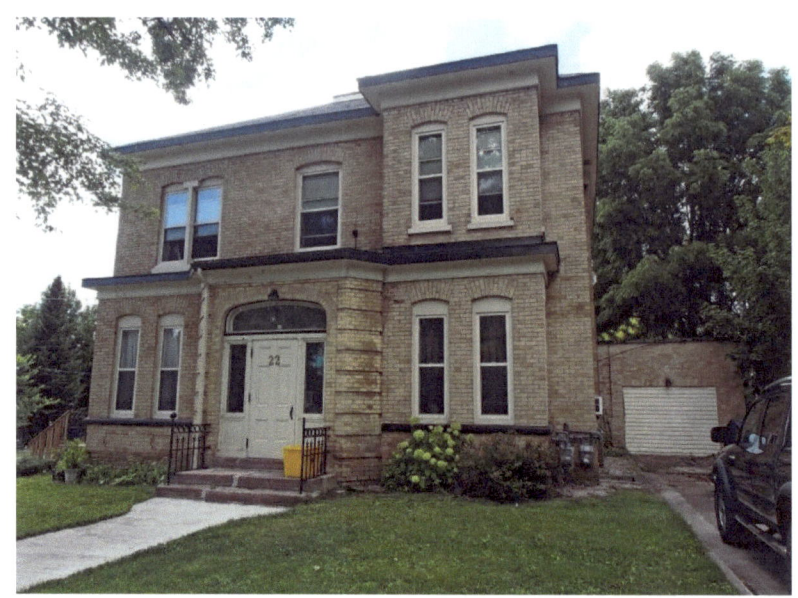

22 Maple Avenue – hip roof, two-storey bay window on the right, one-storey bay window on the left, voussoirs, sidelights and transom window

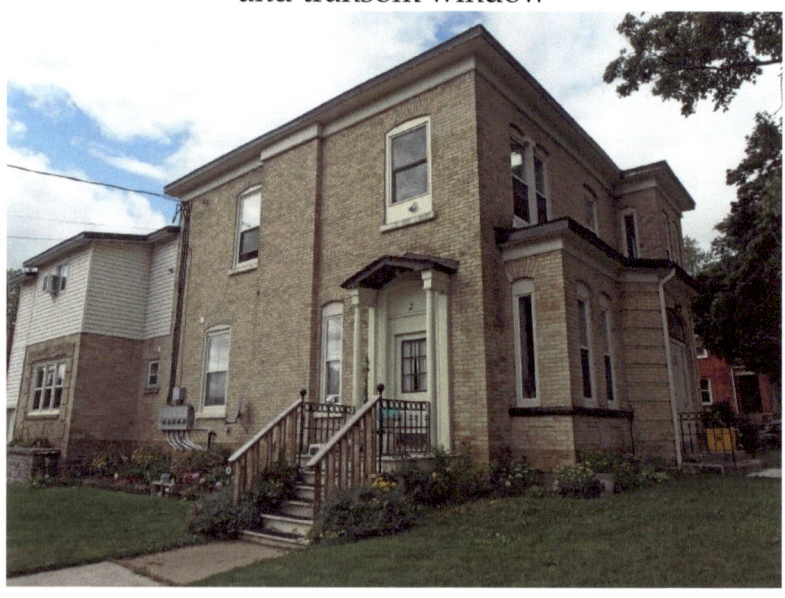

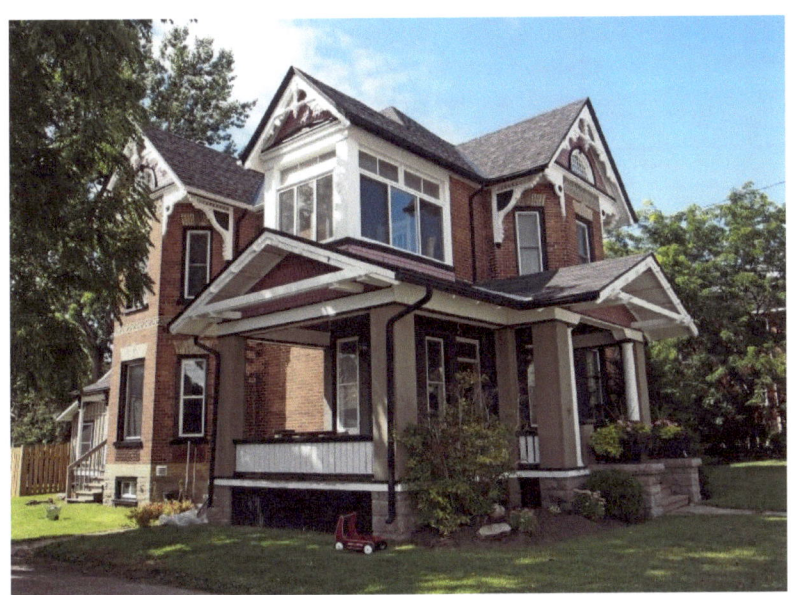

16 Maple Avenue – Victorian Cottage style – c. late 1890s – double bay windows, high gables decorated with detailed wood trim and finials, fretwork, voussoirs and keystones, dichromatic brickwork and banding; upper exterior porch; elegant entrance

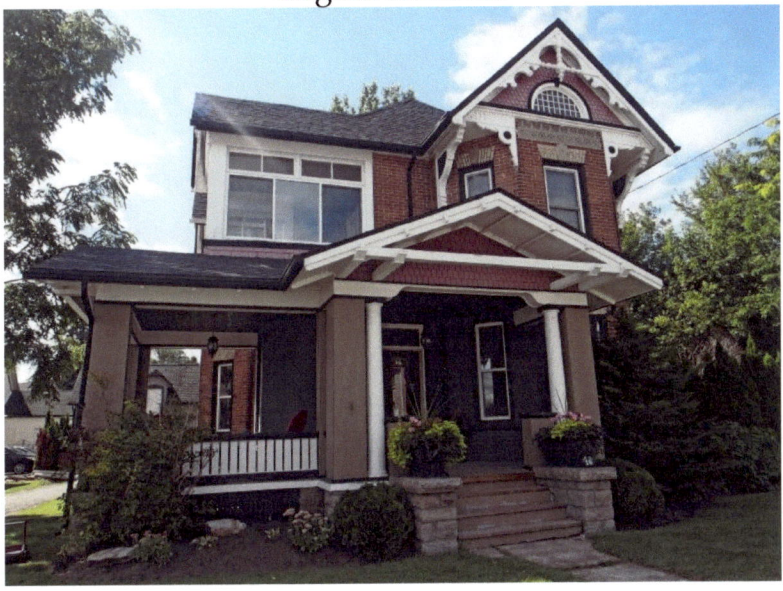

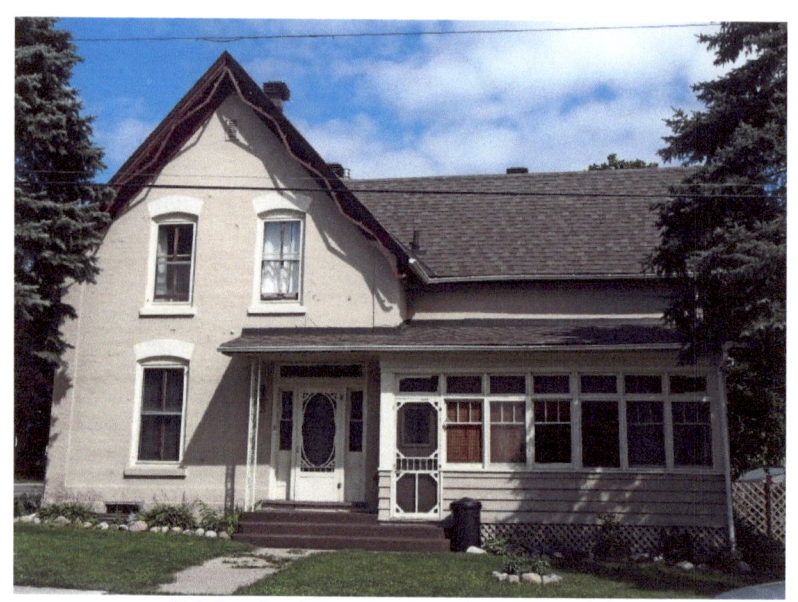

9 Maple Avenue – trim on gable

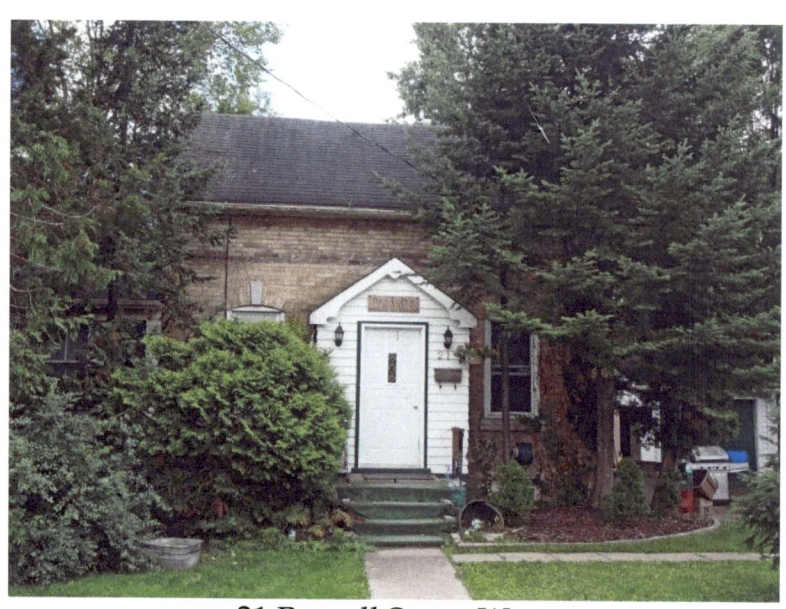

21 Russell Street West

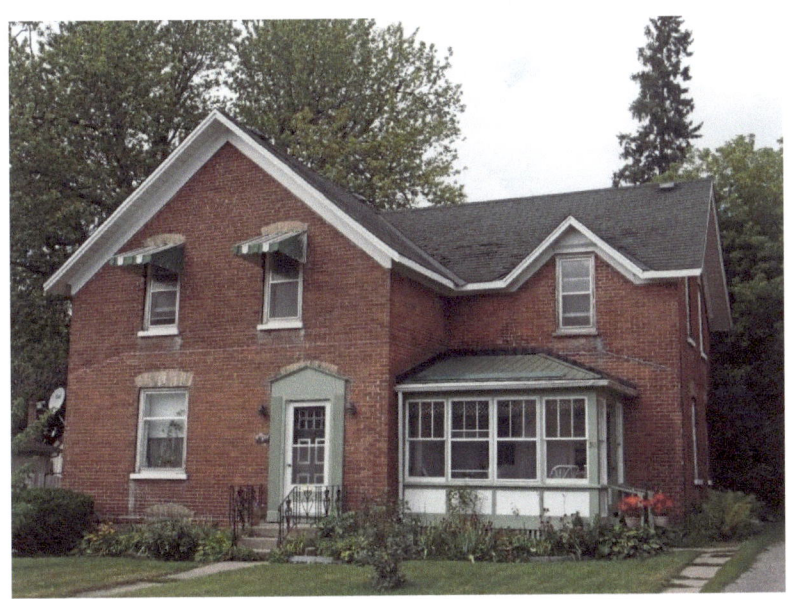

30 Russell Street West – Victorian - voussoirs

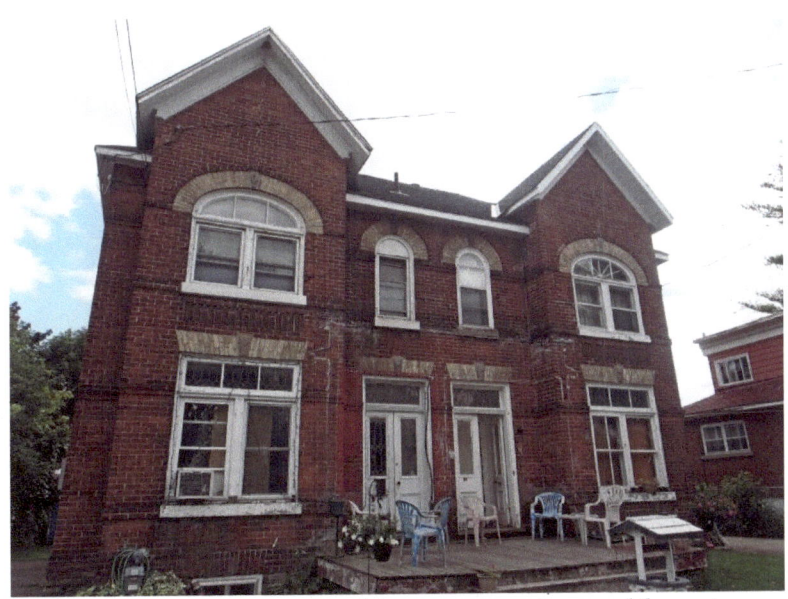

Russell Street West – Gothic – voussoirs and keystones, transom windows

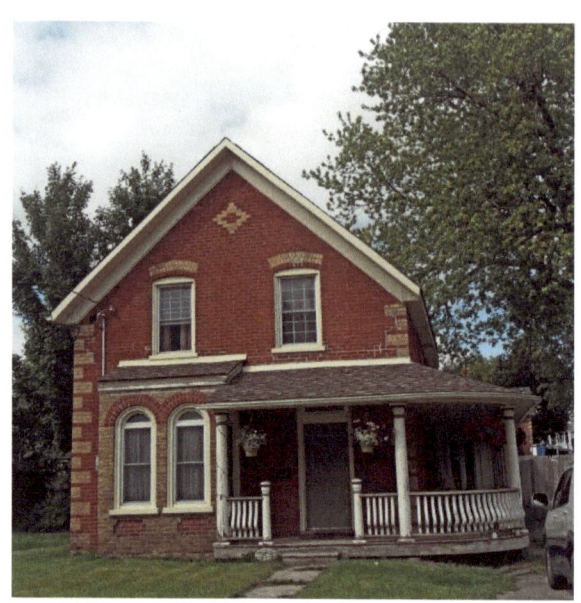

Russell Street West – Gothic – dichromatic quoins, voussoirs and pattern; wraparound veranda

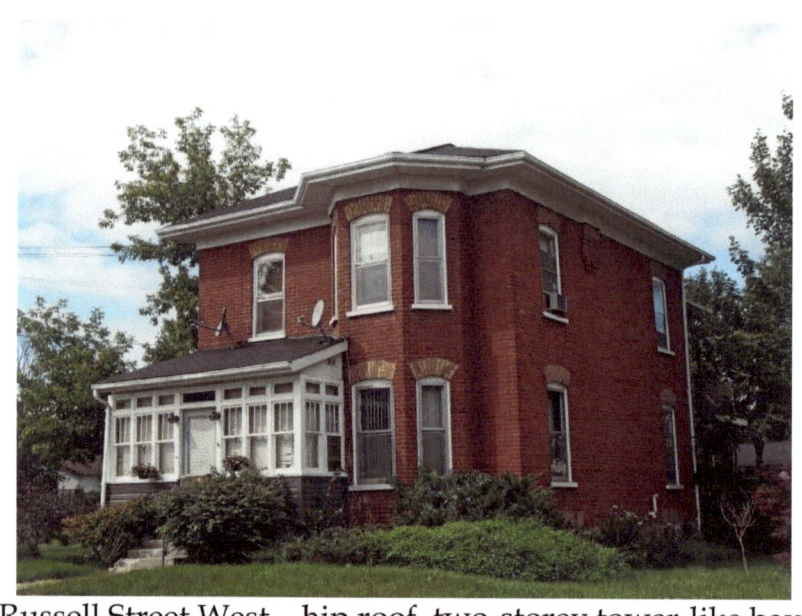

Russell Street West – hip roof, two-storey tower-like bay, voussoirs, enclosed porch

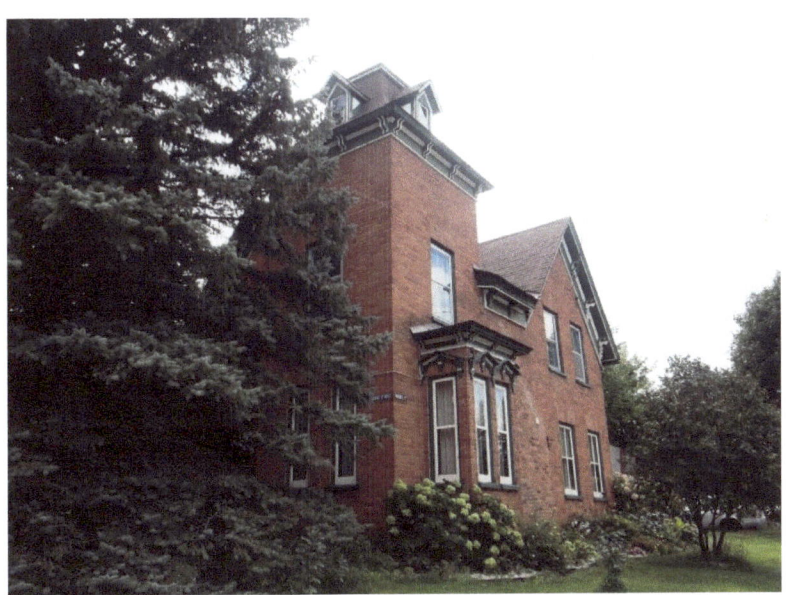

Corner of George and Russell Street West – Queen Anne style
– tower with dormers, bay window with cornice brackets

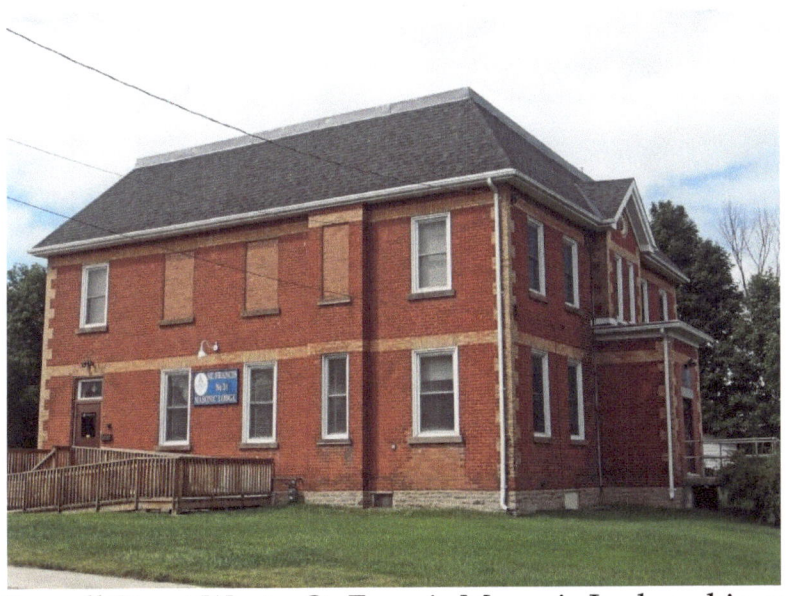

46 Russell Street West – St. Francis Masonic Lodge - hip roof,
banding, corner quoins

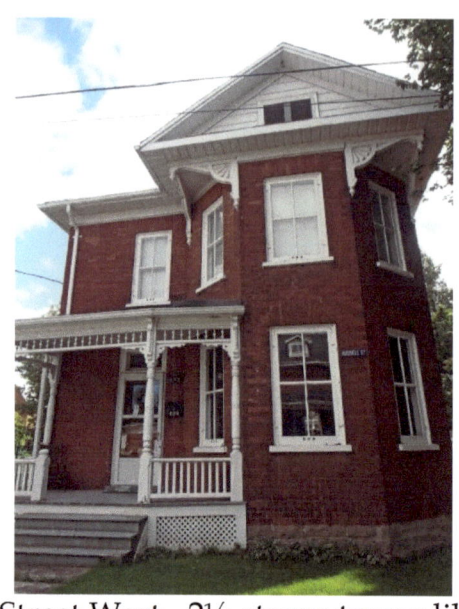

53 Russell Street West - 2½-storey tower-like bay with pediment and fretwork; turned veranda roof supports with decorative capitals and spindles

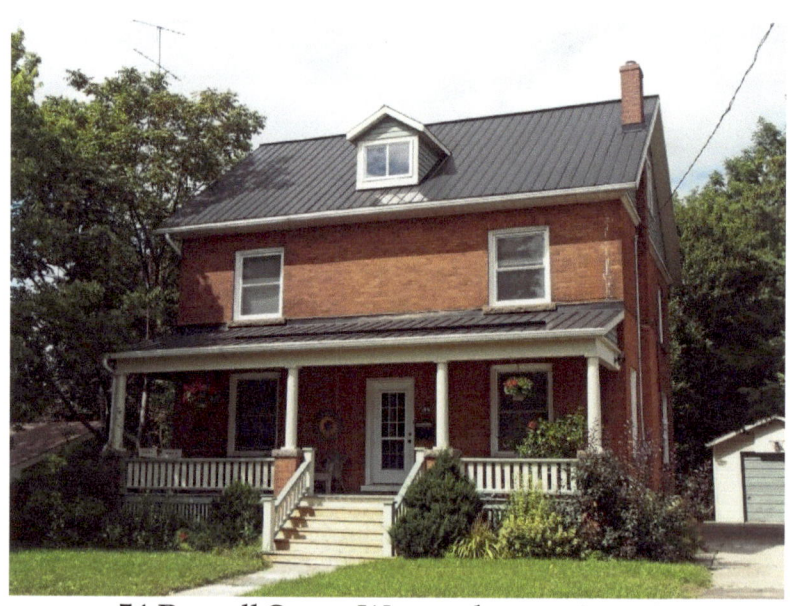

54 Russell Street West – dormer in attic

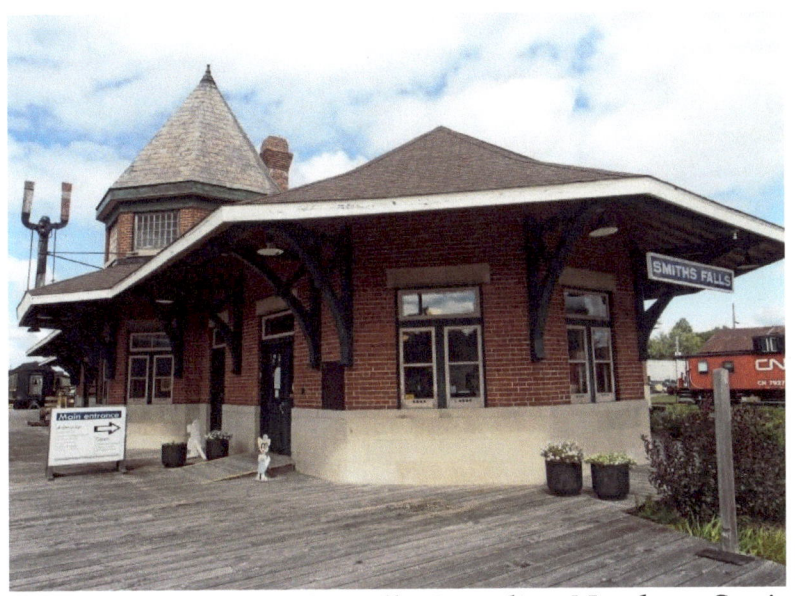

90 William Street – Smiths Falls Canadian Northern Station - 1912

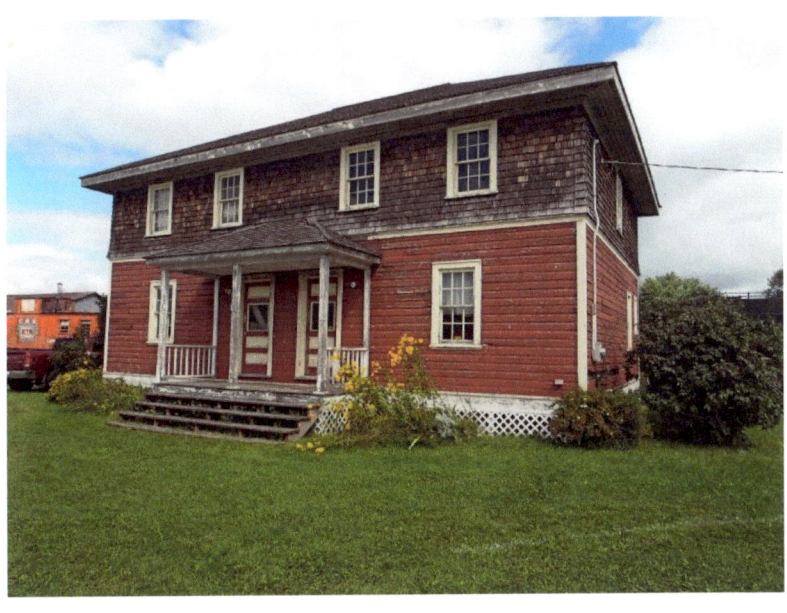

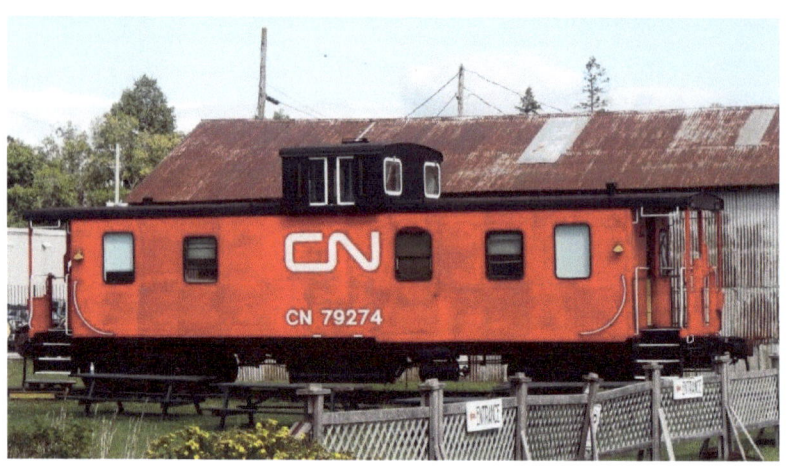

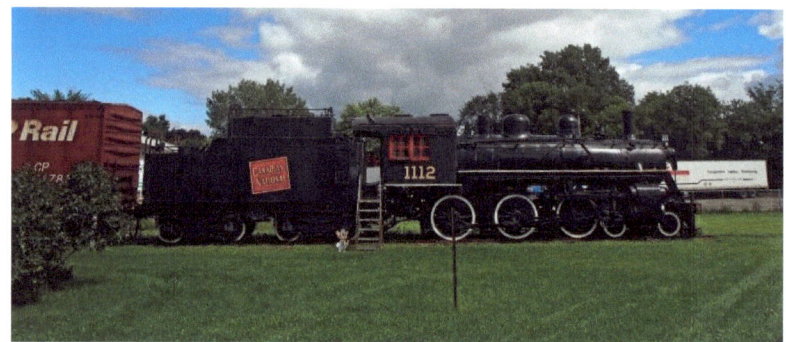

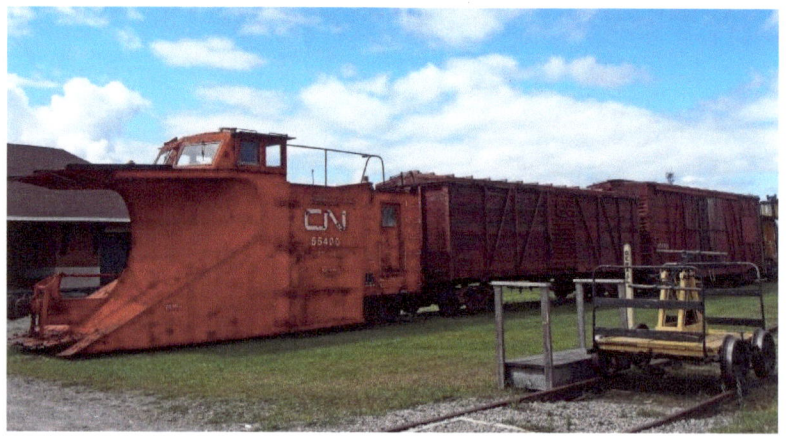

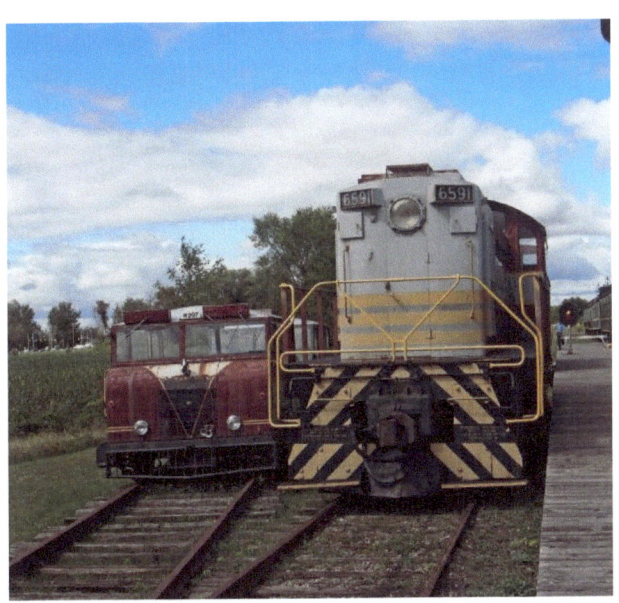

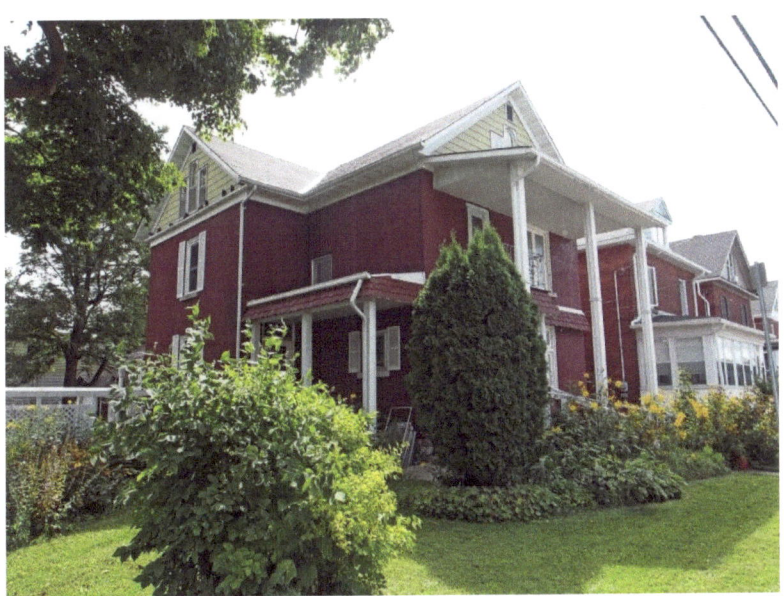

61 William Street – Edwardian – Palladian windows in gables

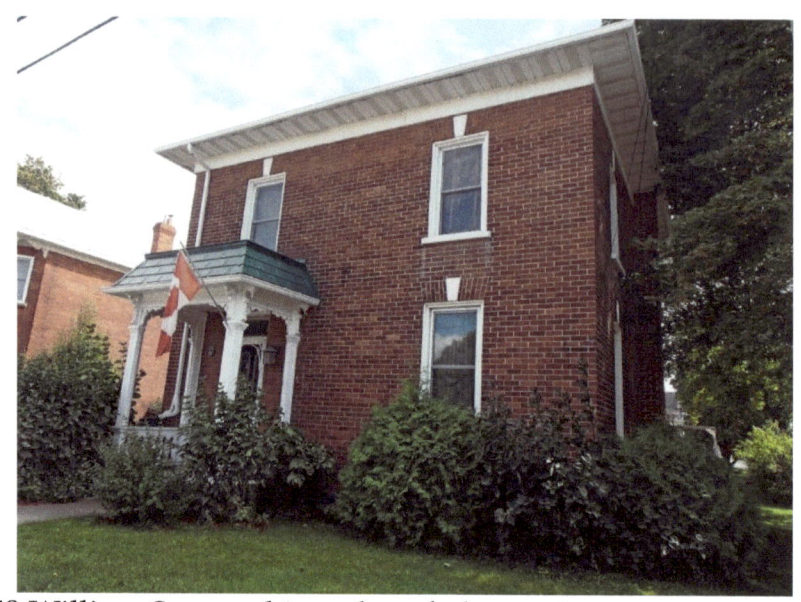

59 William Street – hipped roof, decorative entrance porch

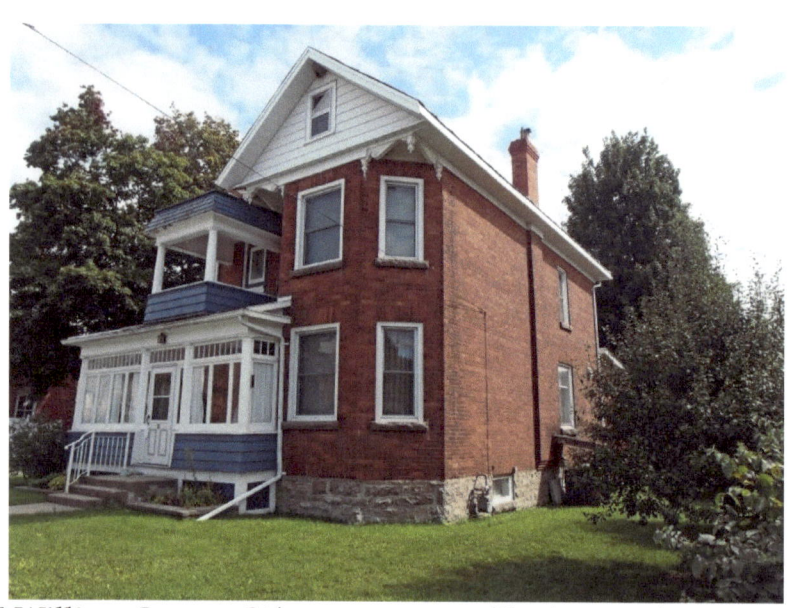

55 William Street - 2½-storey tower-like bay with pediment and fretwork; second floor balcony above enclosed porch

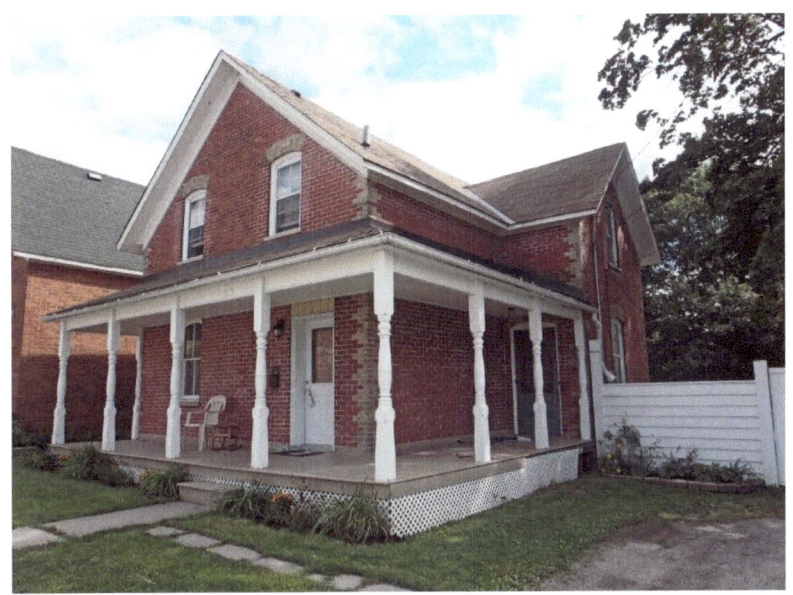

51 William Street - turned veranda roof supports, corner quoins, voussoirs

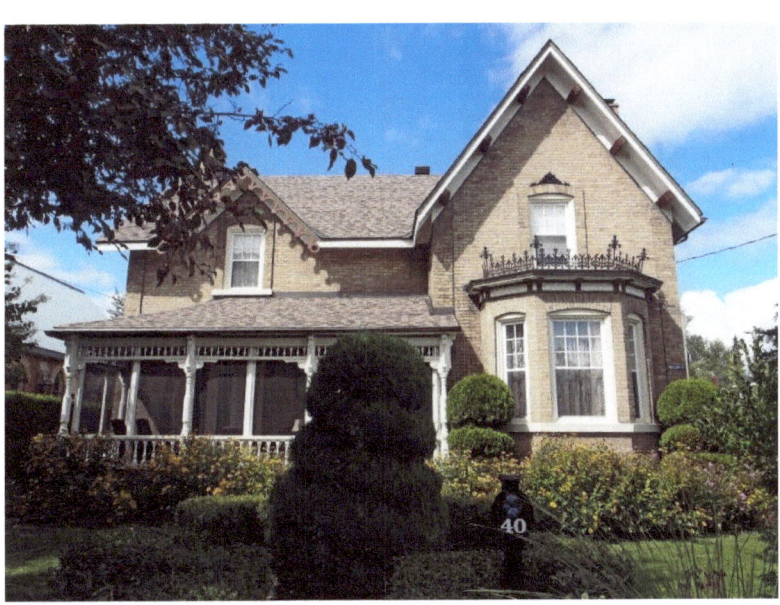

40 William Street – Victorian – iron cresting around balcony above bay window; turned veranda roof supports with decorative capitals and spindles

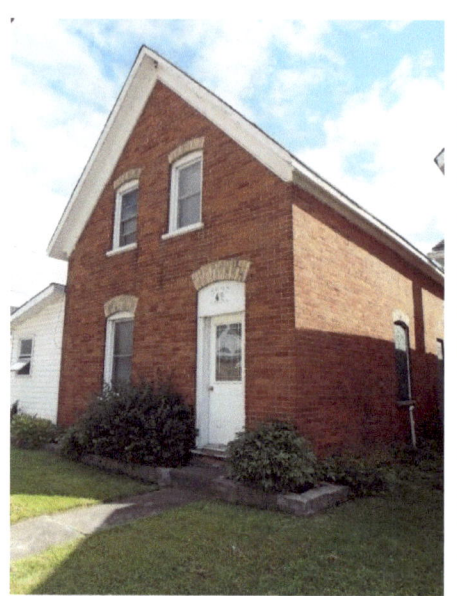

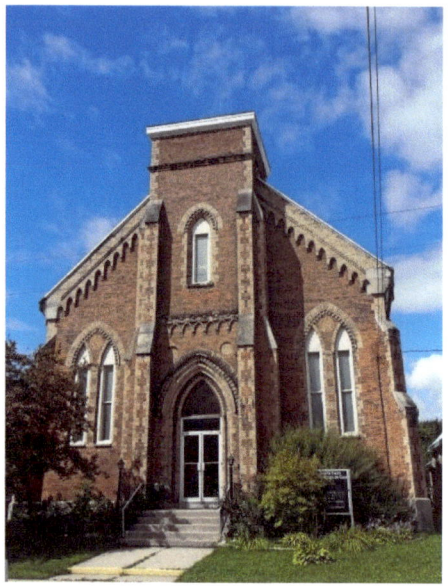

49 William Street
Gothic – voussoirs

Assemblies of God
Gothic – lancet windows,
Buttresses, dichromatic

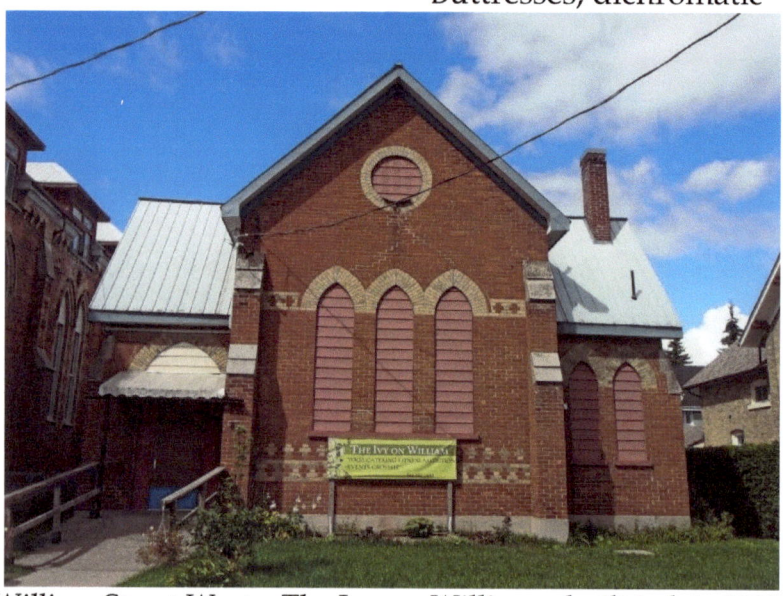

42 William Street West – The Ivy on William – built in late 1800s as
a Sunday School - dichromatic brickwork, lancet blind window
openings

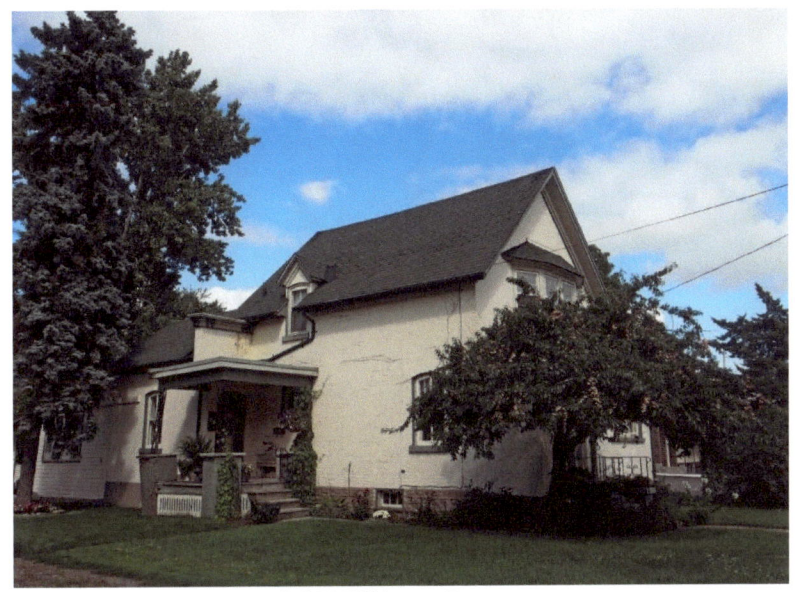

26 William Street

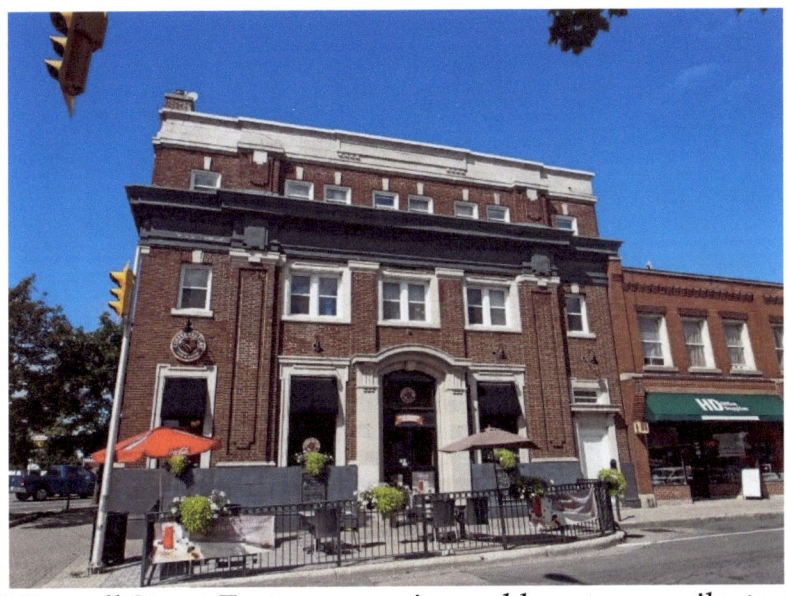

2 Russell Street East – voussoirs and keystones, pilasters

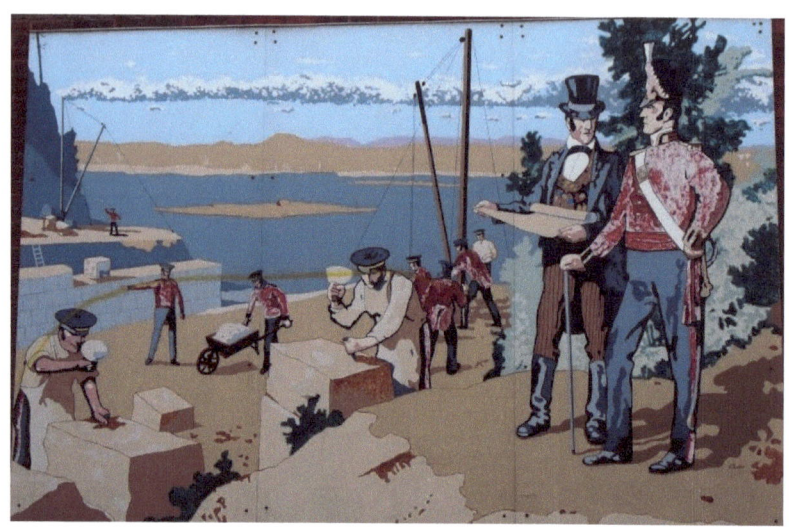

Mural

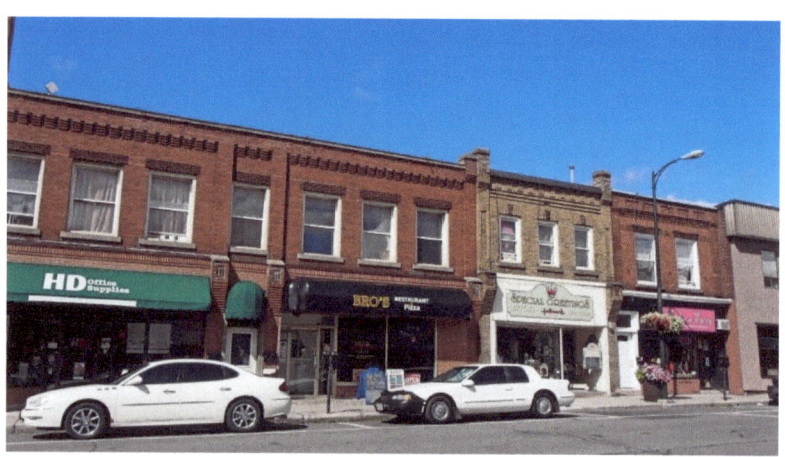

4-10 Russell Street East – bevelled dentil molding; pilasters with corbelling on yellow brick building (#8); saw tooth brickwork on red brick building at far right (#10)

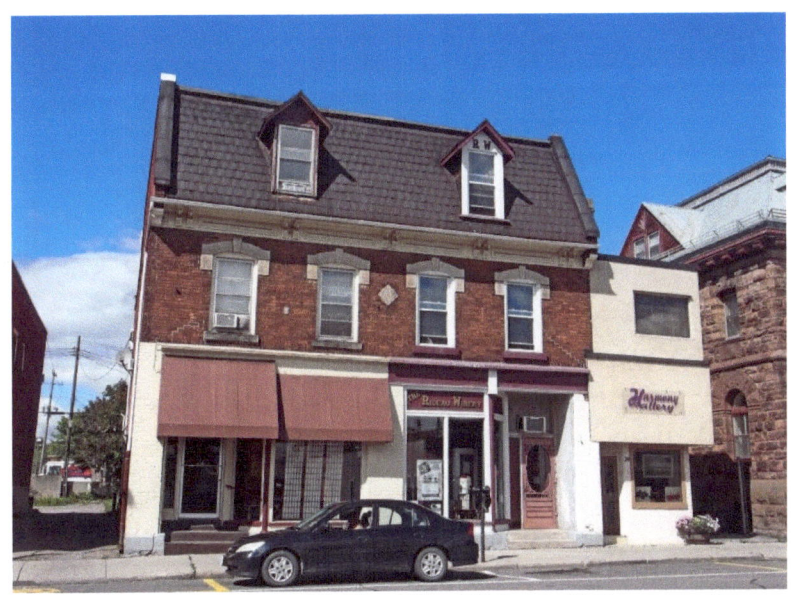

22 Russell Street East – 1887 – The Rideau Winery - dormers, keystones

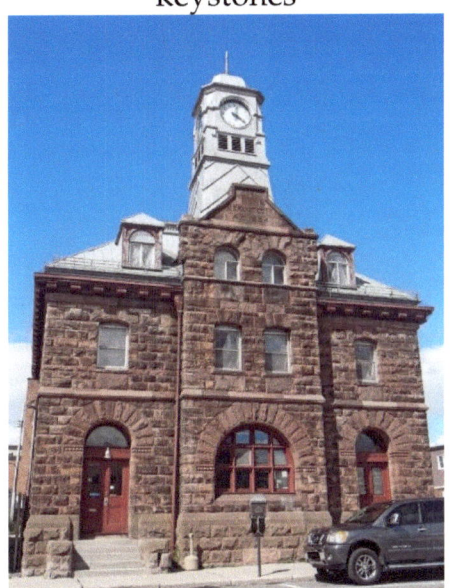

30 Russell Street East – old Post Office – Romanesque style - designed by Thomas Fuller, Dominion Architect, in 1894; clock was added in 1915 – local red sandstone on a foundation of Beckwith limestone with stone trim from Nova Scotia

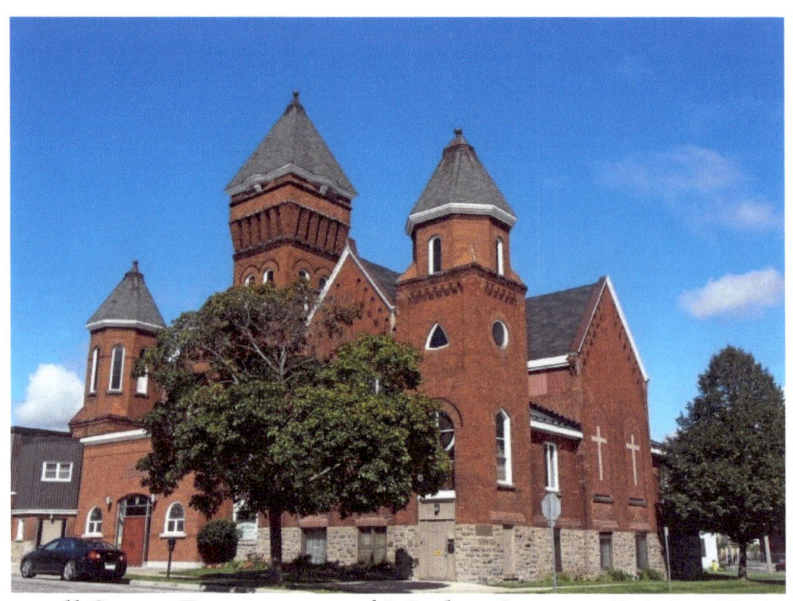

Russell Street East corner of Market Street – Trinity United
Church – 1886 – Queen Anne style – three non-symmetrical
towers, various shaped windows, rose window, bevelled
dentil molding

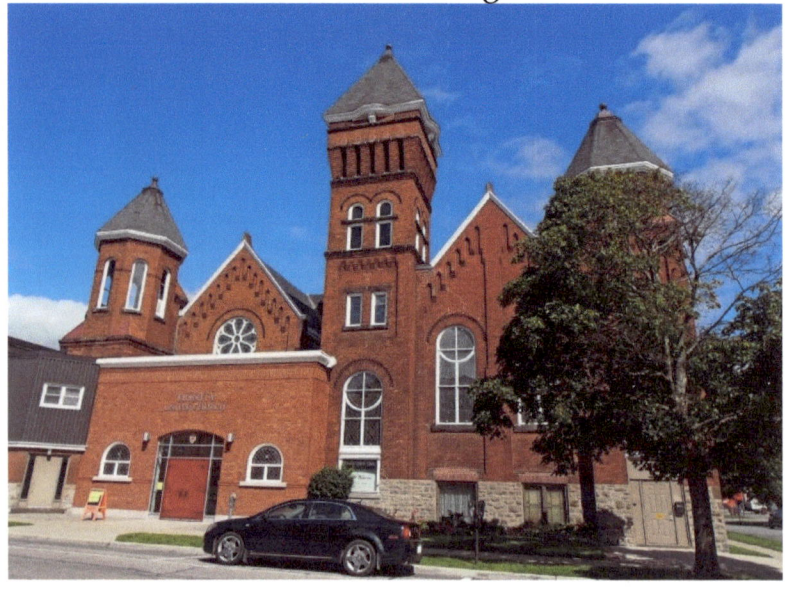

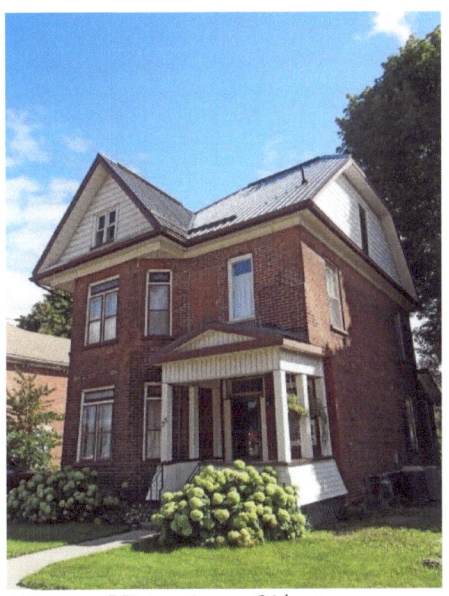

35 Russell Street East – Victorian - 2½-storey tower-like bay with pediment

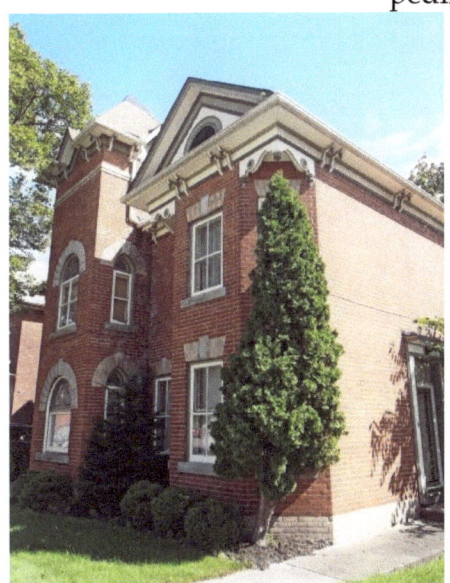
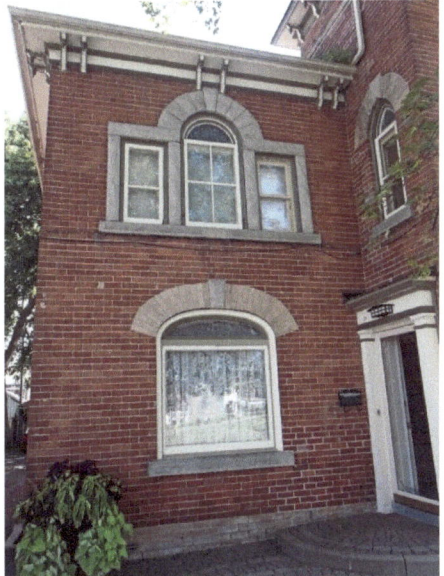

39 Russell Street East – Doctors' House – Italian Villa style – built in 1887 by Charles Cross - square tower asymmetrically placed, with a pyramid-shaped roof with open-centred dormers; stacked angular bay windows to the right of the tower; cornice brackets; front façade with a variety of window styles; dichromatic brickwork

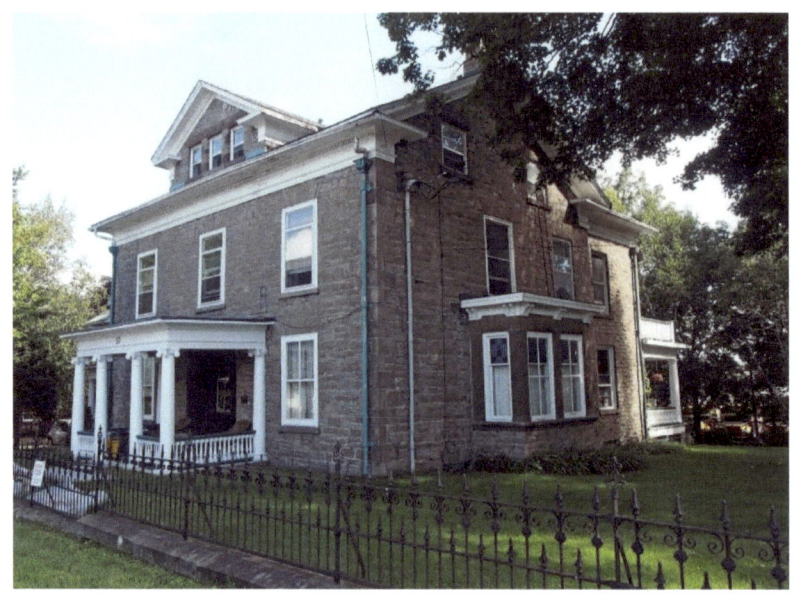

57 Chambers Street – c. 1899 – Neo-Classical house built for Abel Russel Ward who is credited as being the founder of Smiths Falls

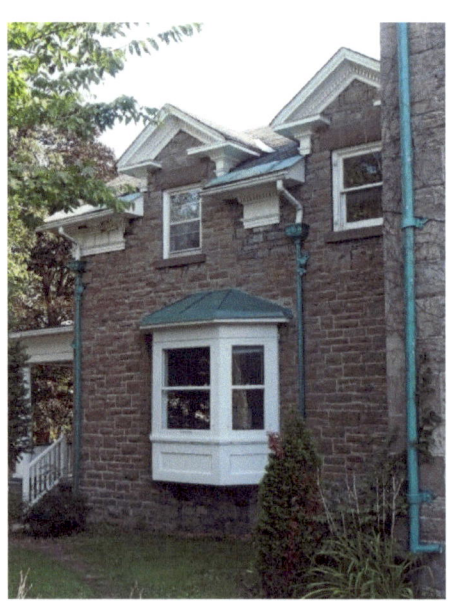

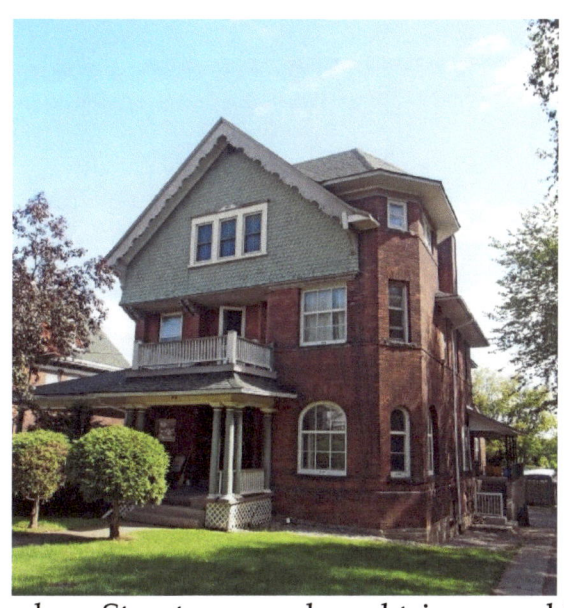

65 Chambers Street – verge board trim on gable with Palladian type window, second floor balcony

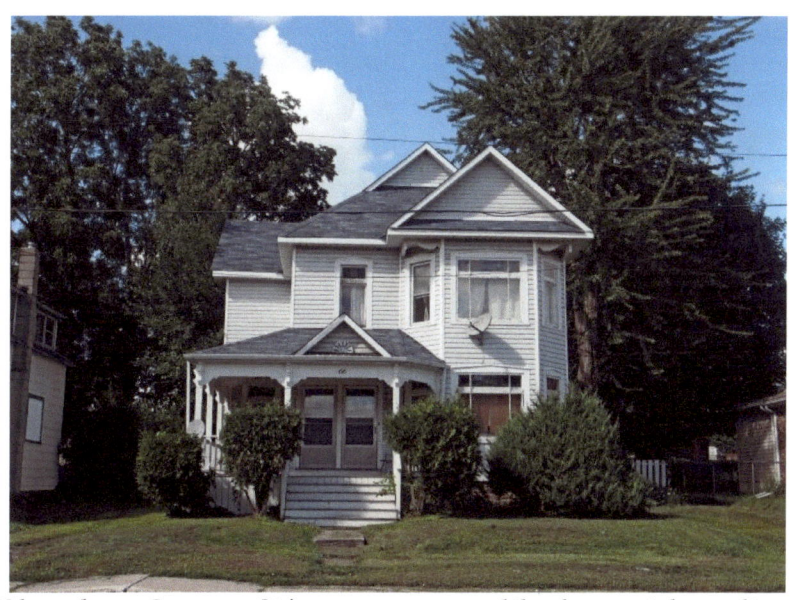

66 Chambers Street - 2½-storey tower-like bay with pediment, fake second pediment behind; pediment above door

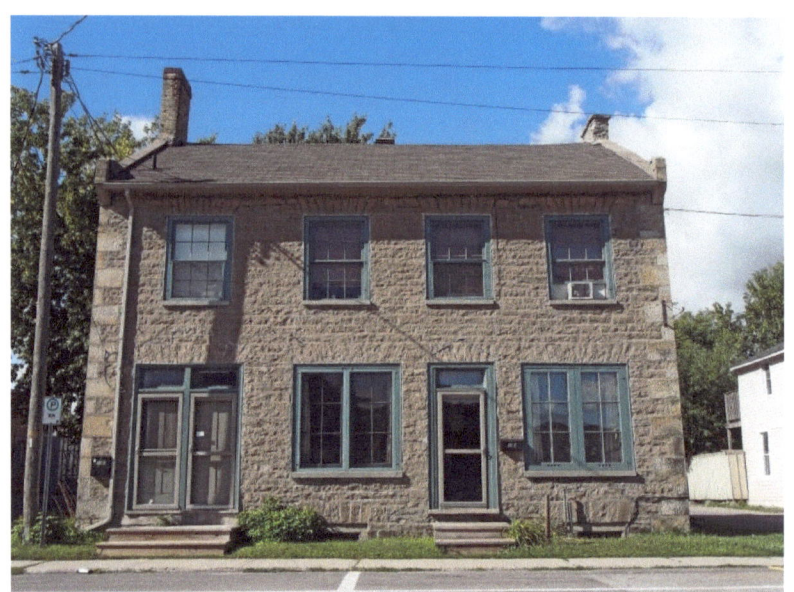

30 Chambers Street – oldest stone building in town – built late 1820s to early 1830s - corner quoins

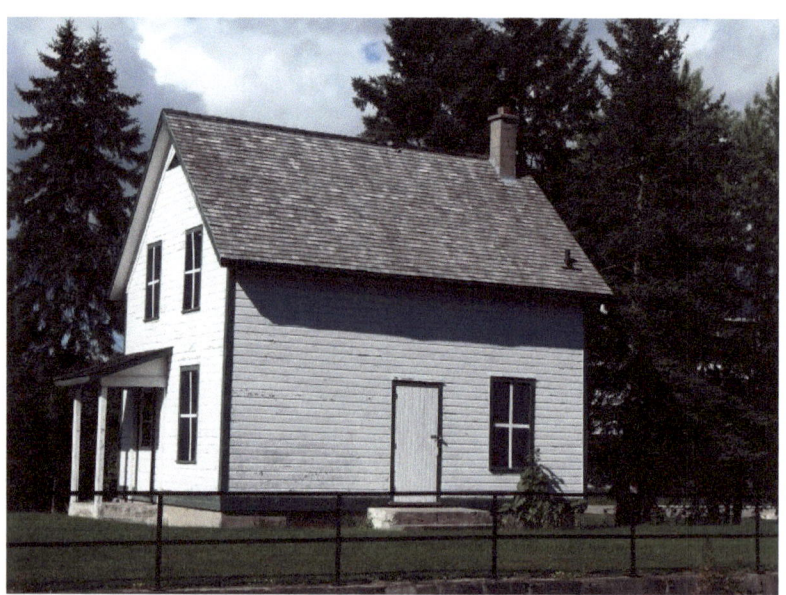

Watch House – 1900 – white frame

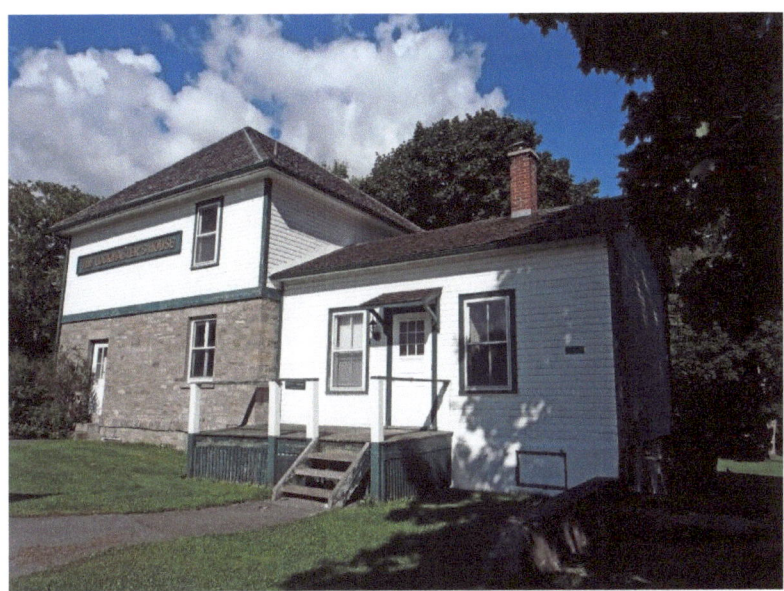

The Lockmaster's House – originally a defensible building built in 1843 – served as residence and office; frame toll collecting office added to right side in 1869; second storey added in 1927. Lock tending was a round-the-clock profession in the early days of the Rideau Canal. The Lockmaster was lock supervisor, record keeper, toll collector, grounds keeper, and public relations man.

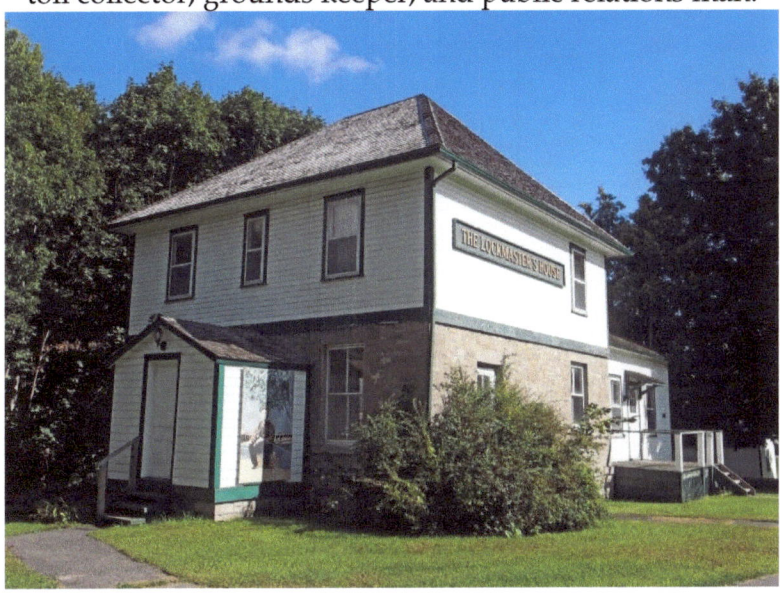

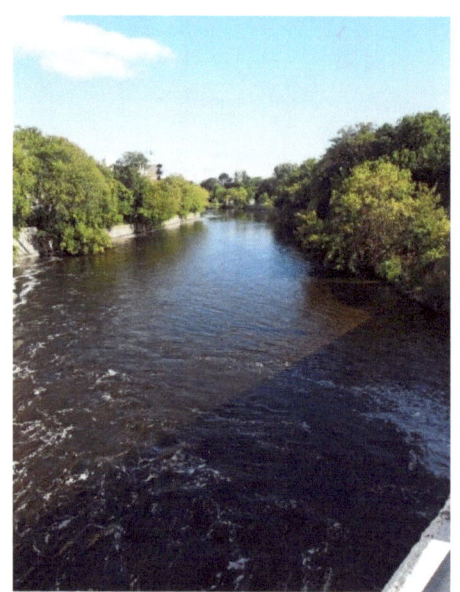

Rideau River

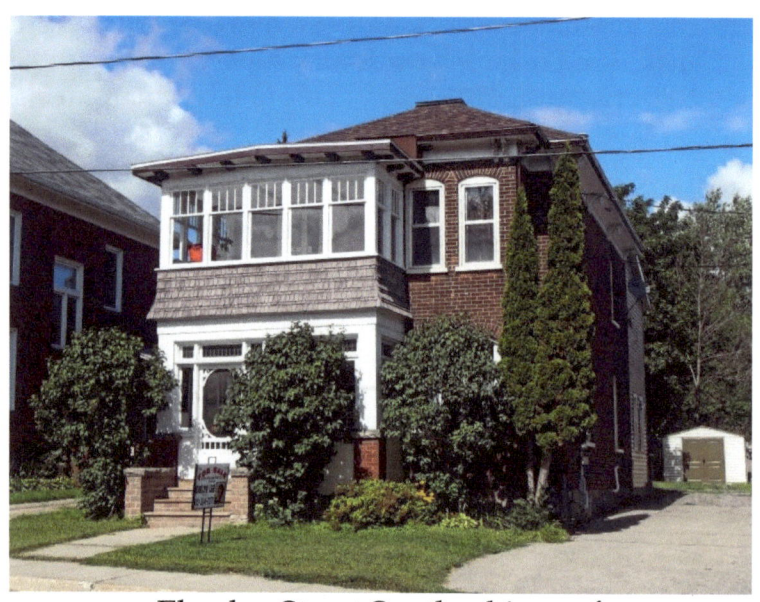

Elmsley Street South – hip roof

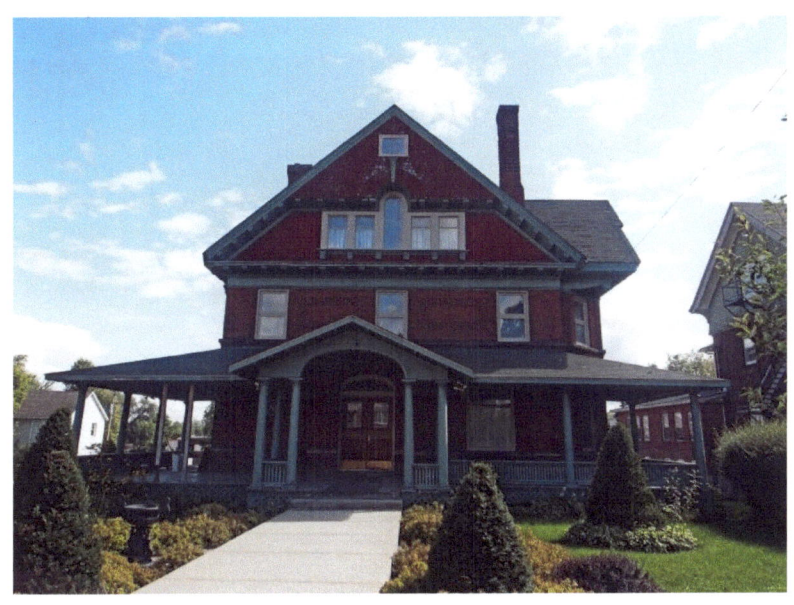

Elmsley Street South – wraparound verandah

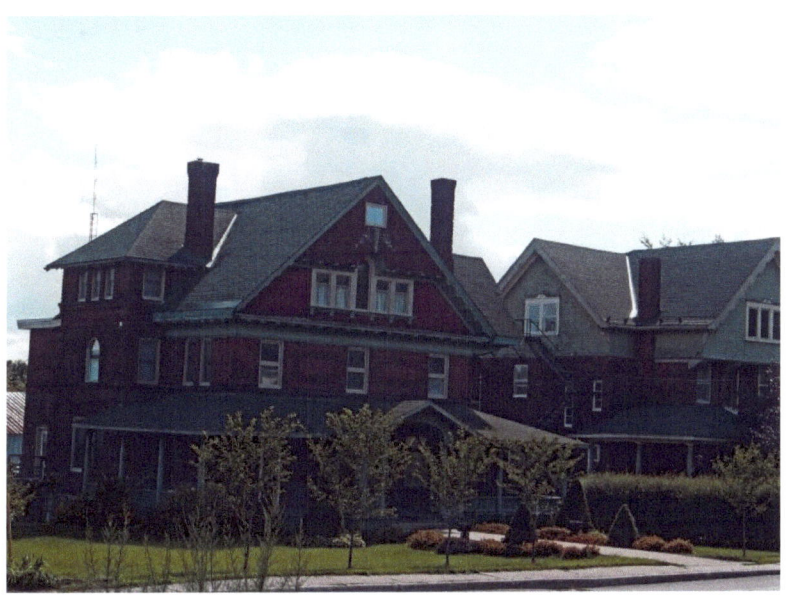

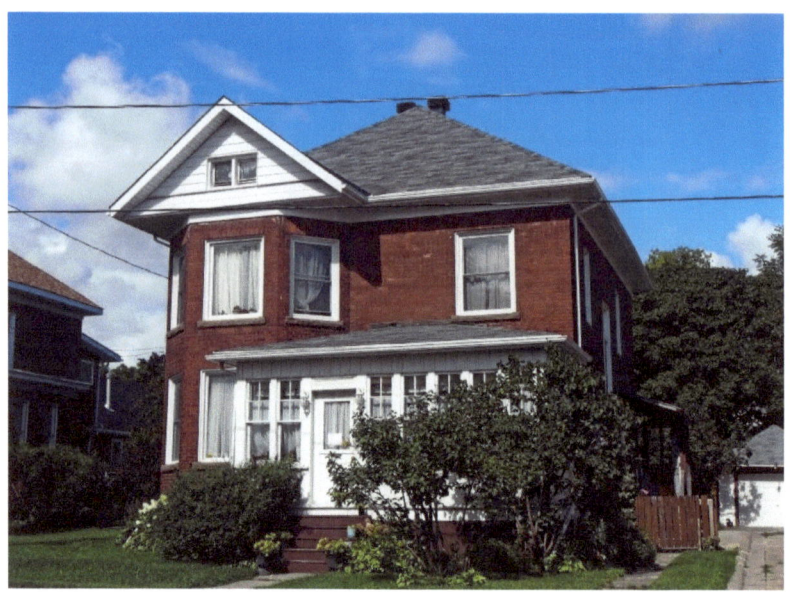

Elmsley Street South – hip roof; 2½-storey tower-like bay with pediment

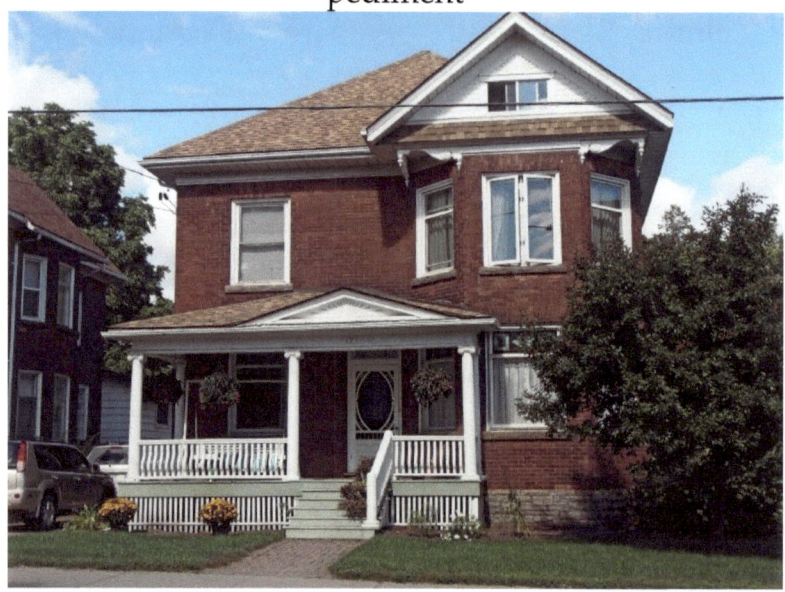

7 Elmsley Street South – hip roof; 2½-storey tower-like bay with pediment; pediment above verandah with Ionic capitals, open railing

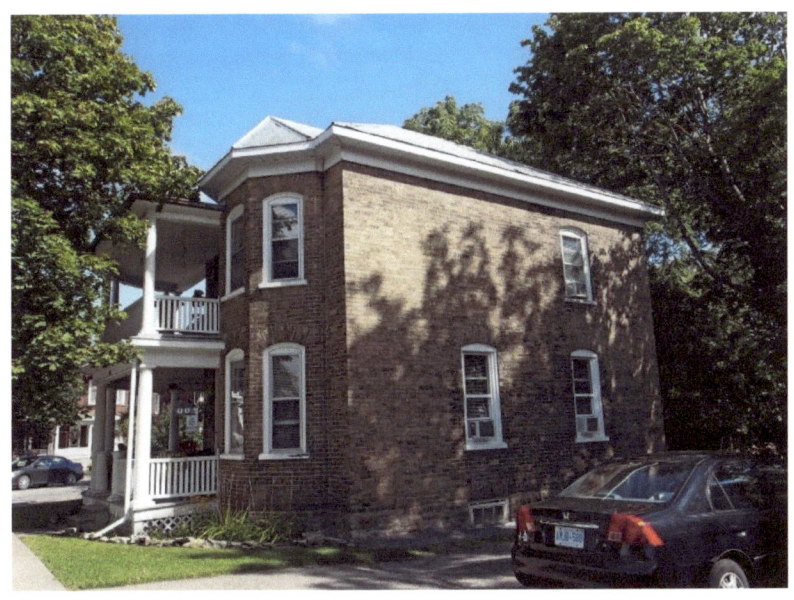

Elmsley Street South

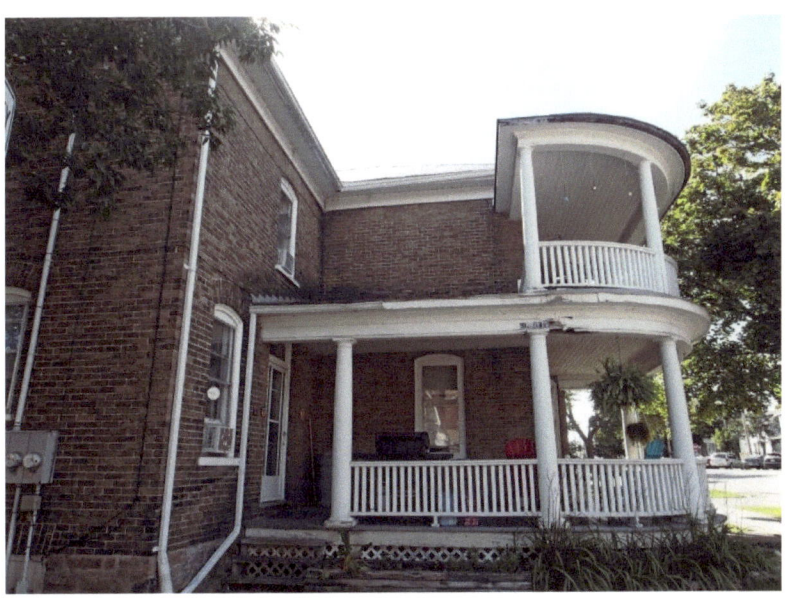

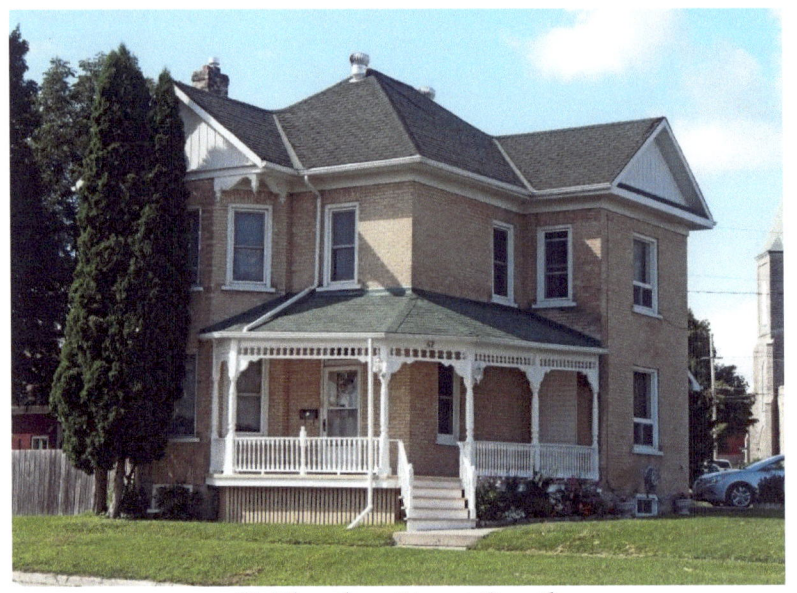

62 Elmsley Street South

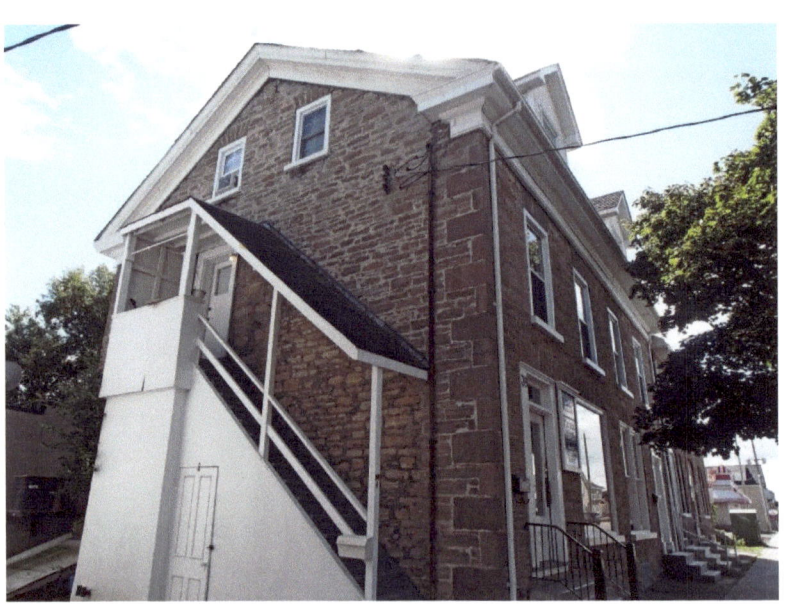

39 Elmsley Street South

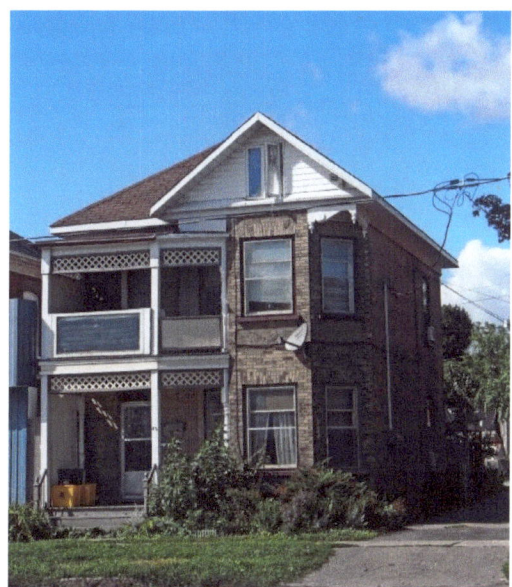

42 Elmsley Street South – fretwork

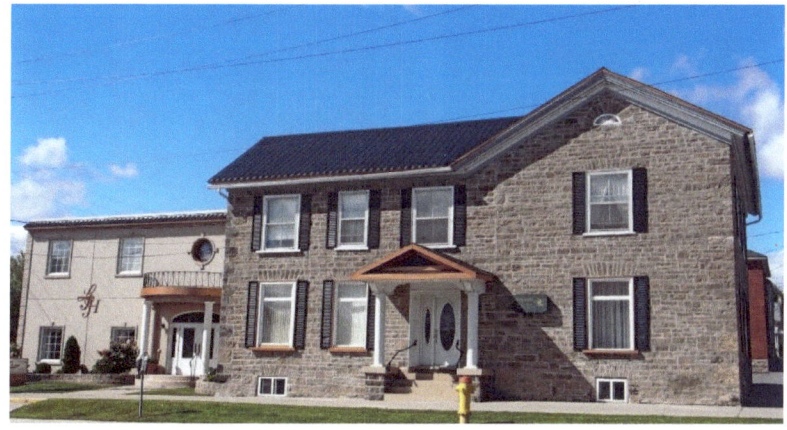

32 Main Street East – originally the Story Hotel, now Lannin Funeral Home and Chapel – Doric pillars below pediment and semi-circular balcony

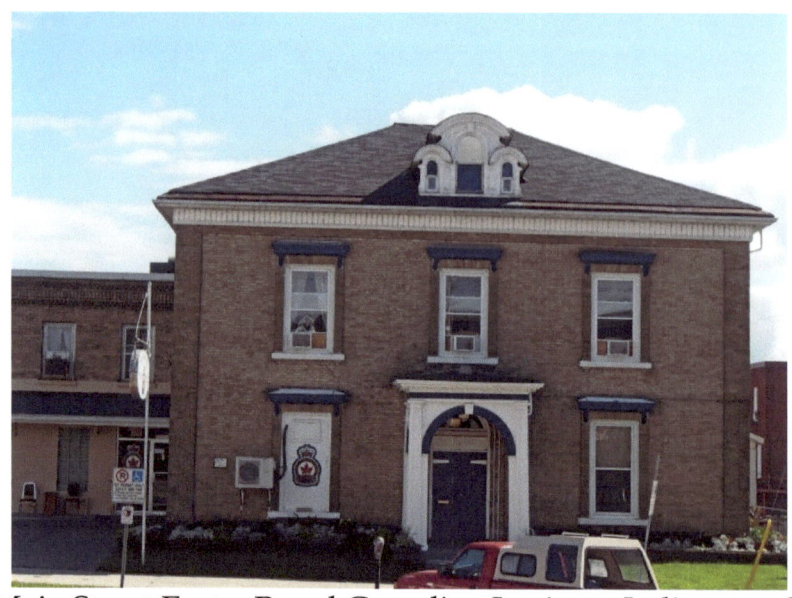

7 Main Street East – Royal Canadian Legion – Italianate - hip roof, ornate dormer, window hoods, entrance

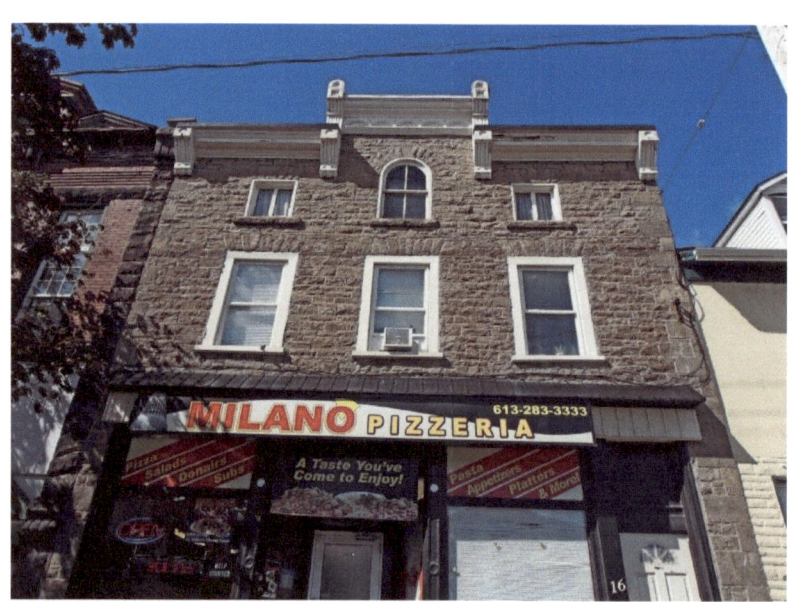

14-16 Main Street East – c. 1843 – Milano Pizzeria – cornice brackets

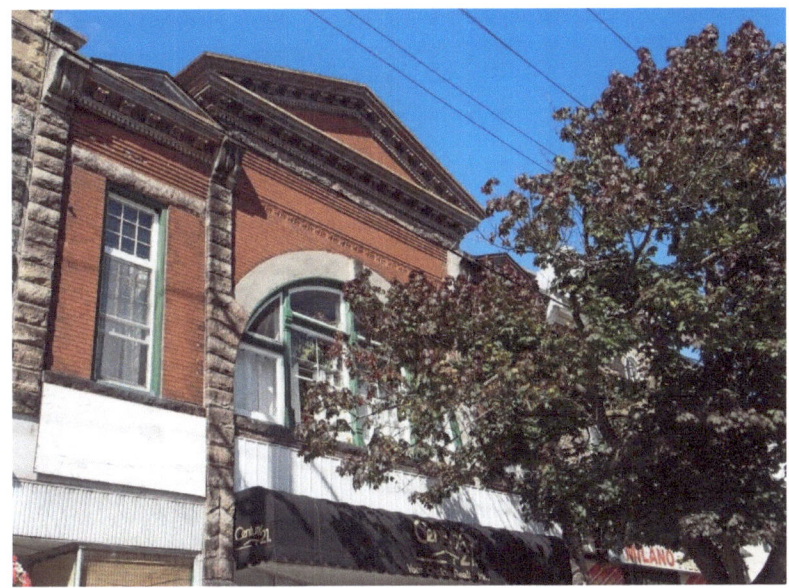

10 Main Street East – c. 1893 – fine brickwork and semi-
circular window – was the Union Bank

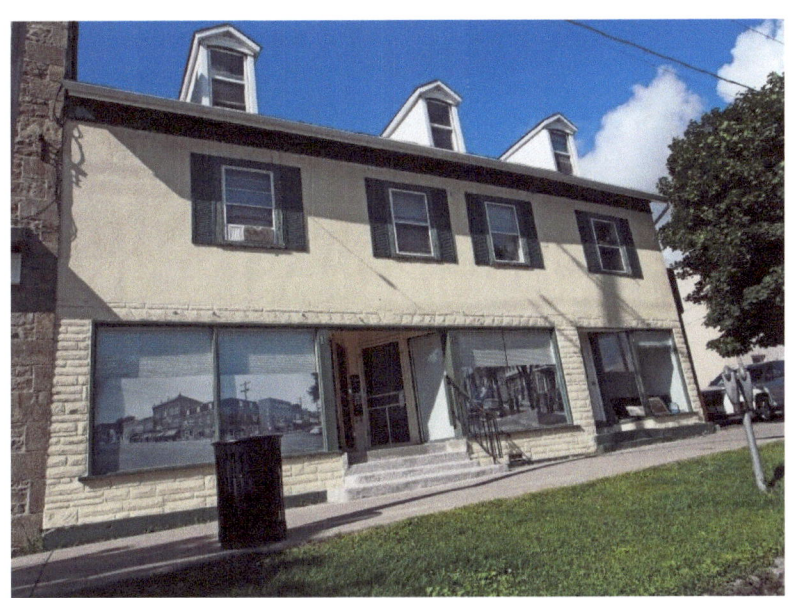

Main Street East – dormers

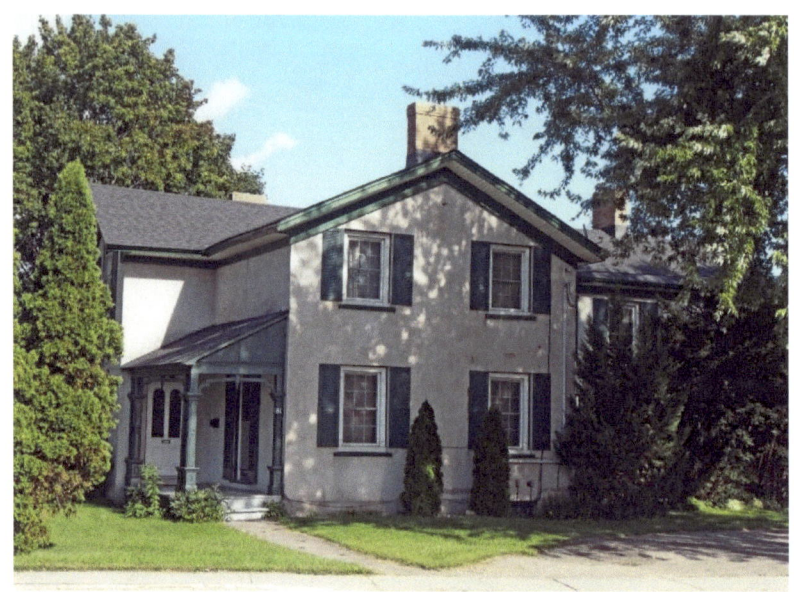

81 Lombard Street

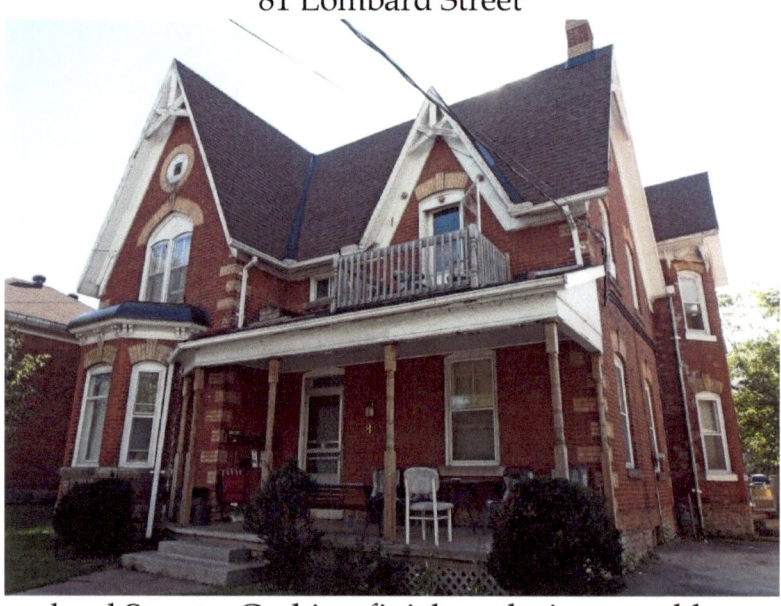

84 Lombard Street – Gothic – finials and trim on gables, corner quoins, voussoirs with keystones, second floor balcony; bay window with cornice brackets; turned spindle roof supports for veranda

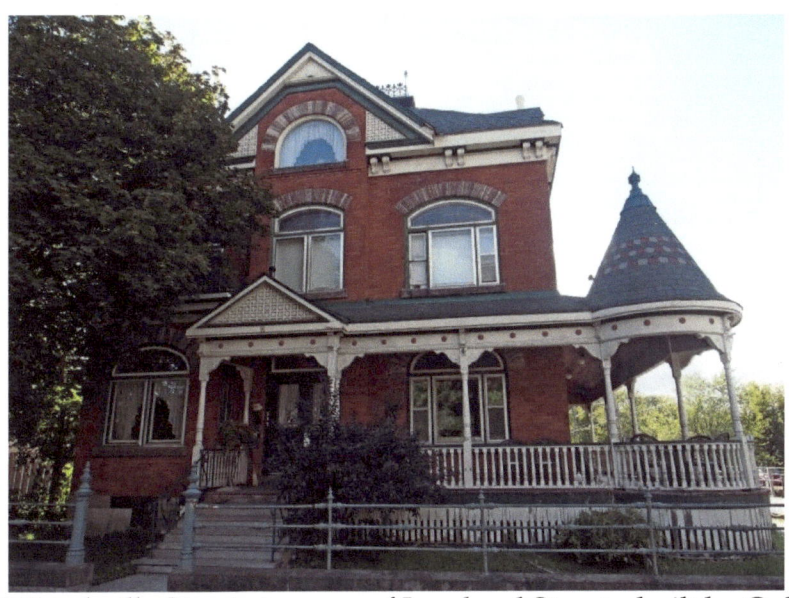

78 Brockville Street at corner of Lombard Street – built by Ogle Carss, an early mayor of the town – 1895 – Queen Anne Revival style – irregular outline, broad gables, multi-sloped roofs, a belvedere, a tower, ornamental cast iron railings on the roof; long, graceful wraparound verandah; stone voussoirs over semi-circular windows with transoms

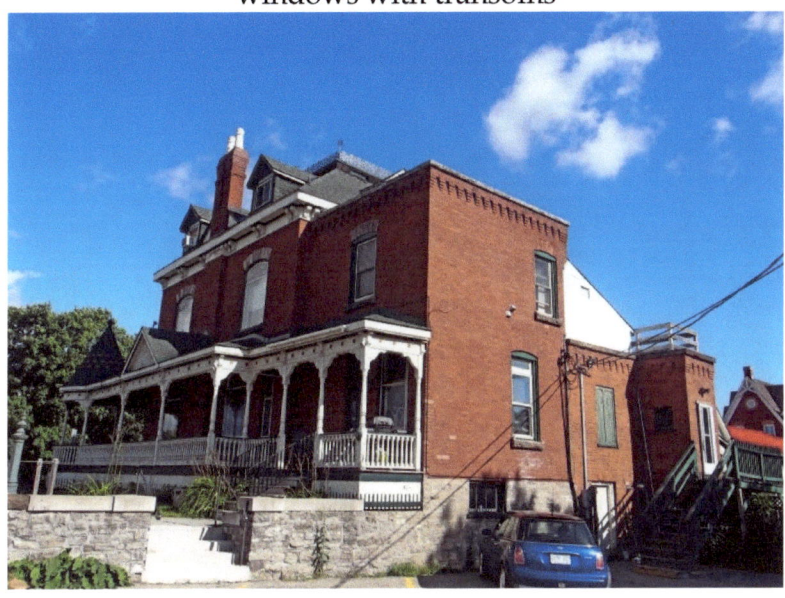

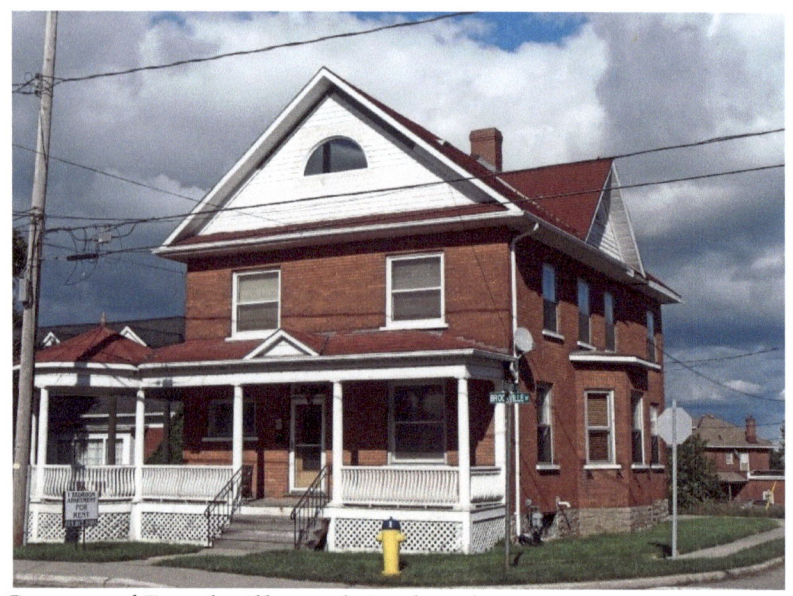

Corner of Brockville and Orchard Streets – Edwardian –
pediment, bay window on side

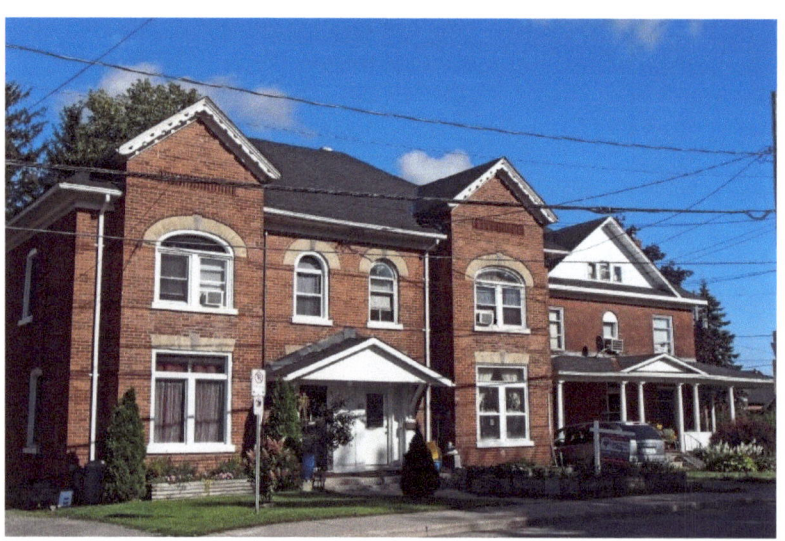

99 Brockville Street – Gothic – verge board trim on gables,
dichromatic voussoirs; 101 Brockville Street – Edwardian –
Palladian window, Doric pillars, pediment

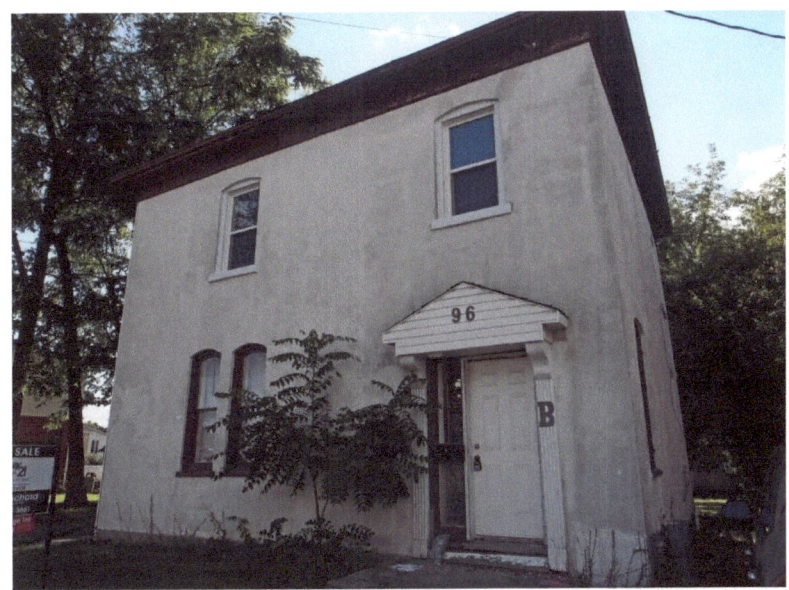

96 Brockville Street

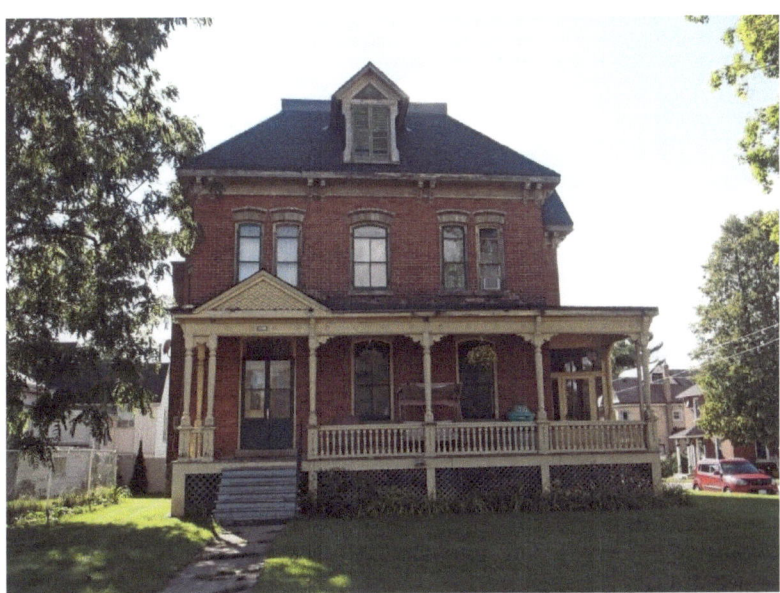

102 Brockville Street – Italianate - steeply pitched hip roof with dormer; cornice brackets, voussoirs; turned veranda roof supports with decorative capitals, open railing; pediment

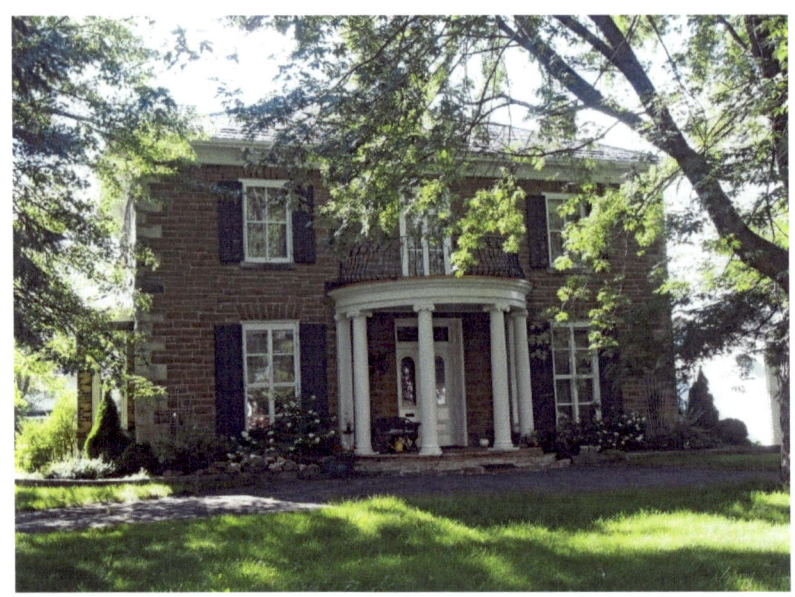

110 Brockville Street – hip roof, corner quoins; semi-circular balcony above open porch with two engaged pillars and four Ionic pillars

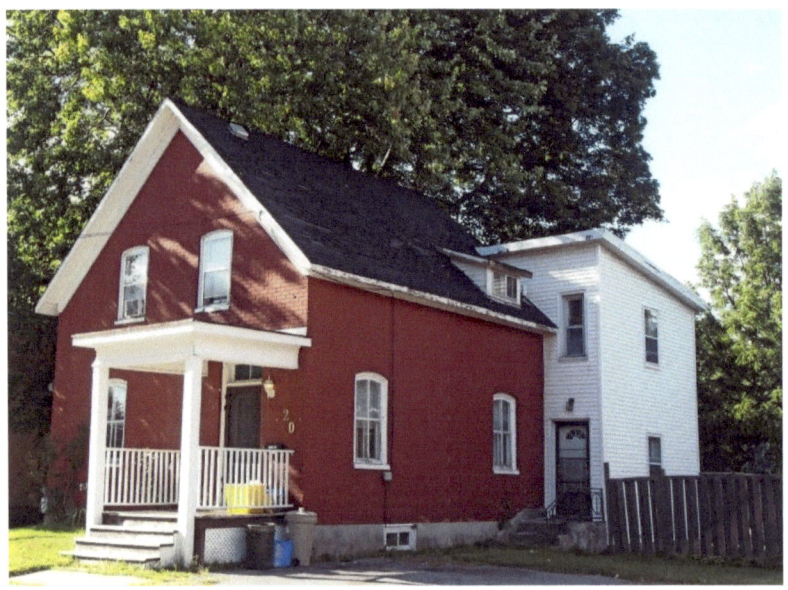

Elm Street - Gothic

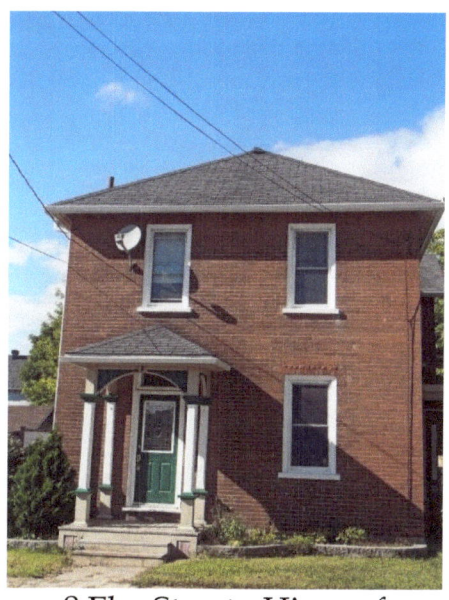

8 Elm Street - Hip roof

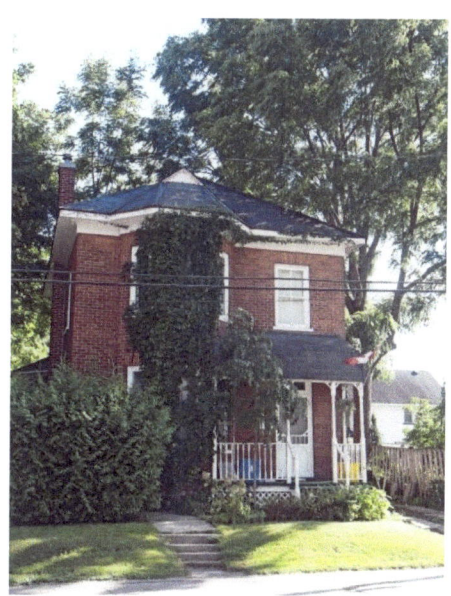
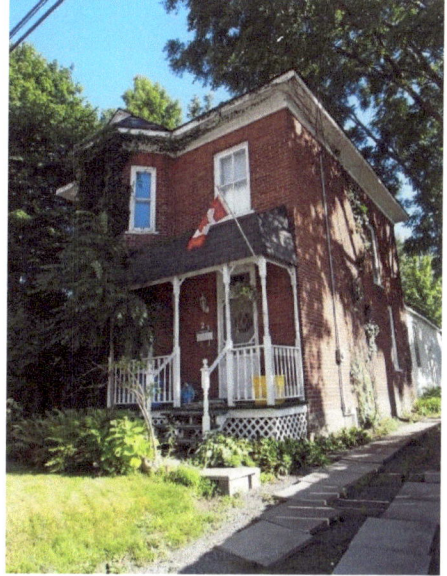

21 Elm Street – hip roof, two-storey bay window

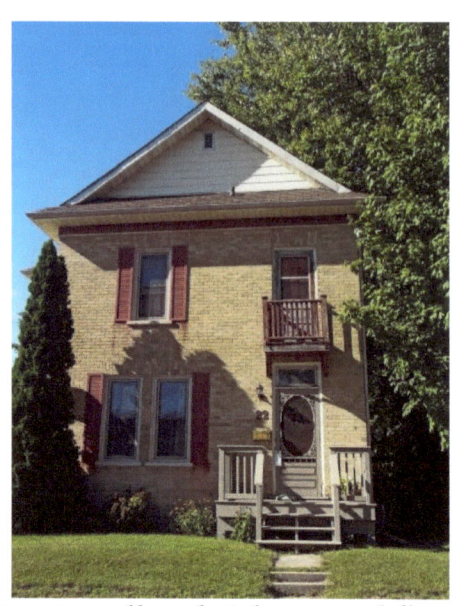

22 Elm Street - yellow brick, second floor balcony

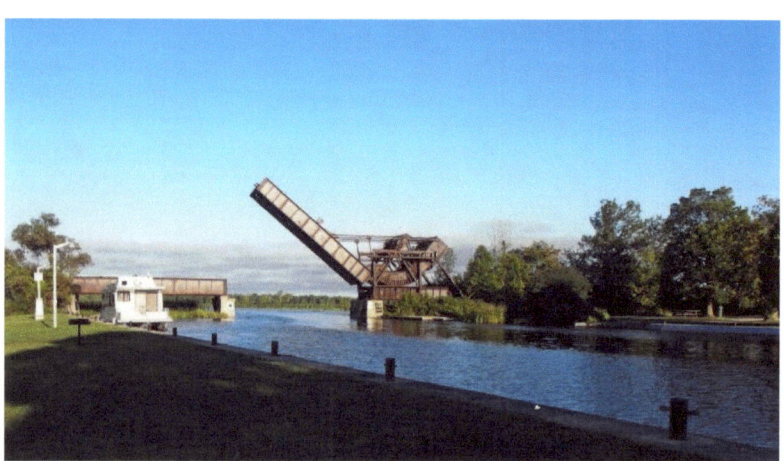

Bascule Bridge – located west of the Detached Locks – a rolling-lift railway bridge built in 1914, now in a permanently raised position – it works like a seesaw – on one end a hinged counter weight drops causing the other end to rise – it was the solution to the point where the railway and canal intersected

Architectural Terms

Banding: A continuous horizontal molding or fascia around a building or on a wall that makes a division in the wall using different materials, colors or textures. Example: 46 Russell Street West, Page 35	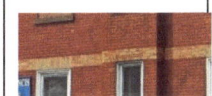
Battlement: A design for a parapet that has alternating solid parts and openings, originally used for defense, but later used as a decorative motif. Example: 11 Church Street West, Page 20	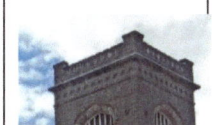
Bay Window: A window that projects out from a wall, in a semicircular, rectangular, or polygonal design. Used frequently in Gothic and Victorian designs. Example: 15 Elmsley Street North, Pay 12	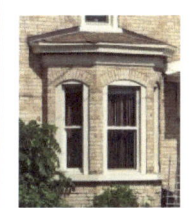
Brackets: a decorative or weight-bearing structural element which forms a right angle with one side against a wall and the other under a projecting surface such as an eave or roof. Example: 14-16 Main Street East, Page 58	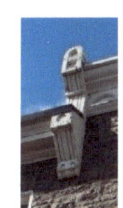
Buttress: a masonry structure built against or projecting from a wall which serves to support or reinforce the wall. In Canadian architecture, they are sometimes used for decoration. Example: William Street, Page 42	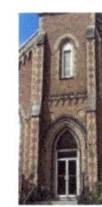

Capital: The uppermost finish or decoration on a column. An Ionic column has a small base, a thin elegant shaft, and a capital composed of volutes which are carved whirls or twists that take the form of a scroll. Example: 81 Beckwith Street North, Page 13	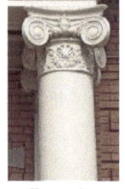 Ionic
A Doric column is characterized by a plain column with no base, a shaft with twenty flutings, and a simple capital with a simple entablature. Example: 99 Brockville Street, Page 62	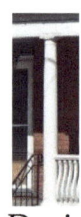 Doric
Corbel: Corbelling is the original method of making arches a series of stones or bricks that protrude beyond the lower level to finally cover the arch. Corbels are used to support cornices, turrets, brackets, ribs and oriel windows. A corbel is also a stone or piece of wood that supports a super incumbent weight. Example: 10 Russell Street East, Page 44	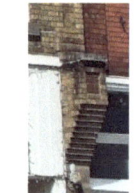
Cornice: originally the wooden overhang of the roof. With the use of stone, brick, iron and steel, the cornice is any horizontal moulded projection at the top of a building. They can be very decorative. Example: 81 Beckwith Street North, Page 13	
Cornice Return: decorative element on the end of a gable. Example: 57 Chambers Street, Page 48	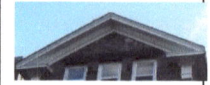

Course: continuous horizontal row or layer of stone or brick. Example: 79 Beckwith Street North, Page 14	
Cupola: A domed or curved roof rising from a building as a decorative element. Example: 79 Beckwith Street North, Page 15	
Dentil Moulding: an even series of rectangles used as ornamental decoration in cornices. Example: 57 Chambers Street, Page 48	
Dichromatic brickwork: the use of two colours of brick, tile or slate to decorate a façade. Example: Russell Street West, Page 34	
Dormer: (French for "sleep") a gable end window that pierces through the plane of a sloping roof surface to create usable space in the top floor or attic of a building by adding headroom. Example: 1 Beckwith Street North, Page 17	
Fretwork: interlaced decorative design resembling a bracket Example: 127 Elmsley Street North, Page 7	

Gable: the triangular portion of a wall between the edges of a sloping roof. Example: 37 Gladstone Avenue, Page 26	
Hip Roof: a roof where all sides slope downwards to the walls with no gables. Example: 17 Elmsley Street North, Page 11	
Iron Cresting: A decorative ornament along the top of a roof. Iron cresting was popular in the Baroque era and also in Italianate, Victorian, Second Empire and Queen Anne styles of architecture. Example: 40 William Street West, Page 41	
Keystones and Voussoirs: a voussoir is a wedge-shaped element used in building an arch. A keystone is the central stone that locks all the stones into position, allowing the arch to bear weight. A keystone is often enlarged and embellished. Example: 84 Lombard Street, Pg.60	
Lancet Window: a tall, narrow window with a pointed arch at its top. Example: 42 William Street West, Page 42	

Mansard Roof: This style was popularized by Francois Mansart (1598-1666), an accomplished architect of the French Baroque period and especially fashionable during the Second French Empire (1852-1870). This roof is almost flat on the top section, with two slopes on each of its sides with the lower slope at a steeper angle than the upper and having dormer windows. Example: Beckwith Street, Page 20	
Palladian Window: a large window that is divided into three sections with the centre section larger than the two side sections and usually arched. Example: 61 William Street, Page 39	
Pediment: a triangular section above the door or portico, usually supported by columns. The inside of the triangle is called the tympanum. Example: 81 Beckwith Street North, Page 13	
Pilaster: a slightly projecting column built into or applied to the face of a wall for additional structural support. Example: 2 Russell Street East, Page 43	
Quoin: masonry blocks at the corner of a wall, often a decorative feature, usually larger or of a different colour than the rest of the wall. Example: 39 Church Street West, Page 24	

Rose Window: a circular window with ornamental tracery radiating from the centre. Example: Russell Street East, Page 46	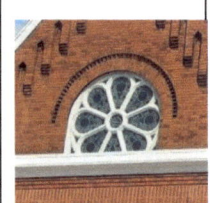
Sidelight: a vertical window that flanks a door, and is often used to emphasize the importance of a primary entrance. **Transom Window:** the light above the doorway, also called a fanlight. Example: 22 Maple Avenue, Page 30	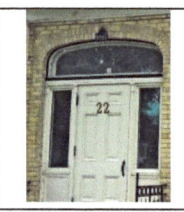
Tower: A circular, square, or octagonal vertical structure higher than the surrounding structure that is usually part of an existing building and is created either for extra defense or for a specific purpose such as a clock or a bell tower. Example: Russell Street East, Page 46	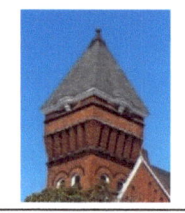
Verge board and Finial: also called bargeboards – hang from the projecting end of a roof and are often elaborately carved and ornamented. **Finial:** ornament added to the top of a gable, pinnacle, canopy or spire – a Gothic element. Example: 65 Chambers Street, Page 49	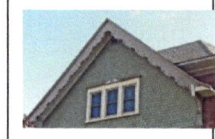
Window Hood: A **hood** is the piece found above window openings, usually of an ornate design, and covers the top third of the opening. Hoods are commonly placed above arched or curved openings on both windows and doors. Example: 7 Main Street East, Page 58	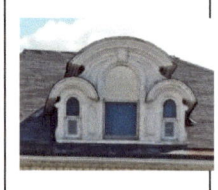

Building Styles

Beaux Arts: Many of the Beaux Arts buildings were banks, post offices, and railway stations. The Ontario Beaux Arts style is eclectic mixing elements of Classical, Renaissance and Baroque. Often the designs have a temple-like façade, porticos with pediments, balustrades, and capitals in many styles. Example: 81 Beckwith Street North, Page 13	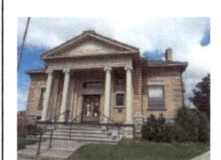
Classical Revival, 1820-1860 – This style was an analytical, scientific, and dogmatic revival based on intensive studies of Greek and Roman buildings, concerned with the application of Greek plans and proportions to civic buildings. Schools, libraries, government offices, and most other civic buildings were built in the Classical Revival style. The white columned porches of the Classical Revival domestic buildings are identified with the mansions of wealthy land owners in Canada. Example: 79 Beckwith Street North, Page 14	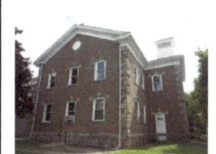
Edwardian, 1900-1930 – This style bridges the ornate and elaborate styles of the Victorian era and the simplified styles of the 20th century. Edwardian Classicism provided simple, balanced facades, simple rooflines, dormer windows, large front porches, and smooth brick surfaces. Voussoirs and keystones are used sparingly. Cornice brackets and braces are block-like and openings have flat arches or plain stone lintels. Example: 61 William Street, Page 39	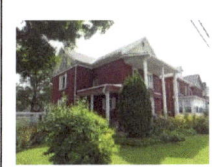

Gothic Revival, 1830-1890 – These decorative buildings have sharply-pitched gables with highly detailed verge boards, pointed-arch window openings, and dichromatic brickwork. It is a common style in Ontario. Example: 84 Lombard Street, Page 60	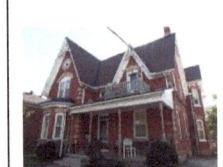
Italianate, 1850-1900 – A two story rectangular building with a mild hip roof, a projecting frontispiece, and generous eaves with ornate cornice brackets was the basis of the style; often there are large sash windows, quoins, ornate detailing on the windows, belvederes and wraparound verandahs. Italianate commercial buildings often have cast iron cresting and elegant window surrounds. Example: 7 Main Street East, Page 58	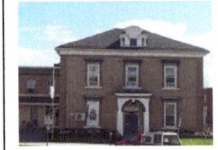
Italian Villa: This style was the first Ontario style that broke from the architectural traditions of the first settlers and imitated the harmony and balance of Classical architecture found in Northern Italian villas. The style is strictly residential and is characterized by an irregular roofline punctuated by a tall tower or campanile (bell tower). Small balconies, cantilevered eaves offering deep summer shade and arcaded porticos are standard features. Architects designing these houses were clearly after the picturesque. Example: 39 Russell Street East, Page 47	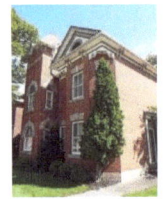

Neo-Classical, 1810-1850 – This style was a direct result of the War of 1812. Many Upper Canadians returning from the war with the United States were second or third generation Loyalists who had inherited land and means from their forefathers. Once the conflict had passed, they had the money and the time to expand their holdings and indulge their architectural whims. Both residential and commercial buildings were constructed on the traditional Georgian plan, but they had a new gaiety and light-heartedness. Detailing became more refined, delicate, and elegant. Example: 57 Chambers Street, Page 48	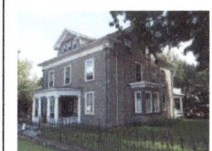
Ontario Cottage - one or one-and-a-half story buildings with a cottage or hip roof. The cottage roof is an equal hip roof where each hip extends to a point in the center of the roof. The hip roof has a long hip in the center. The Ontario Cottage is the vernacular design of the Regency Cottage which generally has a more ornate doorway and a partial or full verandah surrounding it. The roof can have a dormer, a belvedere, and generally two chimneys. Example: 21 Maple Avenue, Page 29	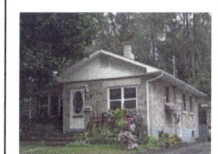
Queen Anne, 1885-1900 – This style is distinguished by an irregular outline featuring a combination of an offset tower, broad gables, projecting two-storey bays, verandahs, multi-sloped roofs, and tall, decorative chimneys. A mixture of brick and wood is common. Windows often have one large single-paned bottom sash and small panes in the upper sash. Example: 78 Brockville Street, Page 61	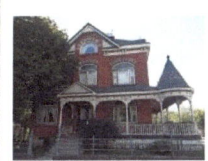

Romanesque Revival, 1880-1910 – This style hearkens back to medieval architecture of the 11th and 12th centuries with a heavy appearance, blocky towers and rounded arches. Example: 30 Russell Street East, Page 45	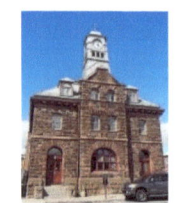
Vernacular/Traditional Mode 1638 - 1950 Influenced but not defined by a particular style, vernacular buildings are made from easily available materials and exhibit local design characteristics. Example: 129 Elmsley Street North, Page 6	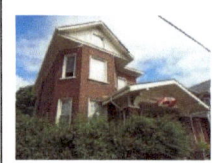
Victorian - In Ontario, a Victorian style building can be seen as any building built between 1840 and 1900 that doesn't fit into any of the other categories. It encompasses a large group of buildings constructed in brick, stone, and timber, using an eclectic mixture of Classical and Gothic motifs. Example: 16 Maple Avenue, Page 31	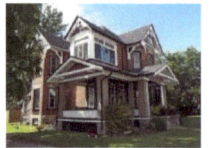

www.ingramcontent.com/pod-product-compliance
Lightning Source LLC
Chambersburg PA
CBHW040833180526
45159CB00001B/173